C. TERRY WARNER

OXFORD
PAPERS

C. TERRY WARNER

OXFORD PAPERS

Edited with an Introduction
by Duane Boyce

The Arbinger Institute

Oxford Papers, C. Terry Warner, was originally published in 1997.

Linacre Prince Edition 2013

Grateful acknowledgment is made of the following original sources reprinted here: "Anger and Similar Delusions," from
The Social Construction of Emotion, edited by Rom Harré, copyright © 1986 by Blackwell, Ltd; "Locating Agency,"
from Annals of Theoretical Psychology, volume 6, edited by Daniel N. Robinson and Leendert P. Mos, copyright ©
1990 by Plenum Publishing; and "The Social Construction of Basic Misconceptions of Behaviour," from El Conocimiento de la Realidad Social, edited by Tomás Ibáñez Gracia, copyright © by Ibáñez and Carto-tec, S.A./
Sendai ediciones.

Copyediting, formatting, and proofreading by Jamie Frost & Michael Rener
Cover Photo by David Iliff CC-BY-SA 3.0

To Alice

Contents

Preface

Educated in philosophy at Yale, C. Terry Warner is professor of philosophy at Brigham Young University and former visiting senior member of Linacre College, Oxford University.

In a steady stream of lectures, papers and seminars over nearly three decades, Warner has presented the results of his academic inquiry into the foundations of human behavior to both scholarly and non-scholarly audiences. This has created substantial demand for written versions of Warner's work. Some have desired non-technical presentations of the material, while others have wanted convenient access to various presentations of the technical philosophical theory itself. Warner's work *Bonds That Make Us Free* (Shadow Mountain Press, 2001) is intended to satisfy the first interest; the sampling of Warner's papers assembled here is intended to satisfy, at least partially, the second.

Because these papers, among others, were all prepared as part of Warner's work at Oxford—either presented in lectures there, or prepared in response to colleagues there—they are loosely categorized at Arbinger as "The Oxford Papers". Hence the title of this volume (as well as the British spellings that appear throughout).

In part or in whole, the papers included here have been published or presented in academic settings elsewhere:

"Anger and Similar Delusions" was originally published in Rom Harré, ed., *The Social Construction of Emotion* (Oxford: Basil Blackwell, 1986), pp. 135-66. "Locating Agency" was originally published in Daniel N. Robinson and Leendert P. Mos, eds., *Annals of Theoretical Psychology*, vol. 6 (New York: Plenum, 1990), pp. 133-45. "Self-deception as Vacuous Experience" appears here for the first time, though parts of it were presented in lectures at the University of Manchester in 1985 and the University of Warwick in 1987. "The Social Construction of Basic Misconceptions of Behaviour" was presented at Universidad Autonóma de Barcelona and Universidad País Vasco in 1987 and was originally published as "La construcción de los errores básicos en la conceptuación de las conductas," in Tomás Ibañez Gracia, ed., *El Conocimiento de la Realidad Social* (Barcelona: Sendai Ediciones, 1988), pp. 85-108. "Irony, Self-deception and Understanding" was originally presented to the Linacre Philosophical Society, Linacre College, Oxford University, October, 1986.

Although these papers are more technical than extant popular treatments of Warner's work, none of them attempts to supply a summary of the theory per se. Each paper is informed by the full theory, and in one form or another expresses it, but none attempts to explicate the theory beyond the requirements of the particular paper. For this reason it was seemed that a systematic presentation of at least the central thread of Warner's theory may be useful to the reader, and such an introduction appears at the beginning of this volume.

I express appreciation to those who have helped with this project. Paul Smith and Jim Ferrell have provided constant encouragement and assistance, and Kimberly Patterson has helped significantly with many editorial matters. My wife, Merralee, assists on all my projects, and once again her help has been invaluable. Alice Johnson has contributed deeply to everything I have done in the years we have worked together, and in more than one way this book would not exist without her. This volume is dedicated to Alice. Finally, I thank Terry for his friendship over more than twenty years; his exemplary character, even more than his genius, has been a constant gift to me.

A final note: Warner has consented in broad concept to a collection of his papers, but since then has had no involvement in the volume's creation or design, or even its direction. From an editorial standpoint the book could not be less his; all editorial decisions, and whatever errors may appear, are solely my responsibility.

Duane Boyce
Editor

Introduction to
Warner's Work

Warner's philosophical work explores the possibility that we humans are in large part self-deceived about what kind of beings we are and why we act as we do, and the quality of living available to us if we can bring our self-deceptions to an end.

To say that we might be self-deceived is to say that our beliefs about ourselves and about each other are more than merely false. They are instead falsifications—distortions of our experience for which we ourselves are responsible. In other words, we are failing, both individually and as a culture, to understand ourselves—not because of an inability to do so, but because of a willful refusal to do so. Our whole way of being—the fundamental manner in which we regard ourselves and others—is a systemic and deep-seated deception of ourselves by ourselves.

This is not a narrow subject. What Warner calls self-deceptive attitudes are the ethical affective and cognitive bases of all types of human unhappiness. These attitudes include despising what we find ourselves repeatedly doing; feeling overcome by, and helpless in the face of, abuse suffering from enmity, bitterness, vengeance, or fear—indeed, every emotion or mood in which we feel provoked, used, victimized, disturbed, or in some manner overcome. Such attitudes express the conflictedness, defensiveness, anxiety, or compulsivity, which lies at the heart of the misery suffered by those who hold such attitudes.

To embark on a theory of this scope is to rival Freud. Whereas Freud assumed that we arrive at complex models of human nature due to our psychological complexity as human subjects, Warner has asked whether these models are not instead a function of our duplicity or self-deception as inquirers. If so—and the case he makes is a compelling one—we are never going to be able to understand the corruption of experience called self-deception unless we are free from self-deception. The self-understanding of human beings turns out to be not merely a scientific project, but even more fundamentally an ethical one. The result is that what starts out in Warner's work as a technical exploration of the logical puzzle of self-deception explodes before very long into a sweeping examination of the ethical and ontological character of being human.

Since it is impossible in a brief overview to do justice to the depth and technical elegance of Warner's work, I will not attempt to do so. Instead, my purpose is merely to isolate the central thread of Warner's argument and to track its major points of development in the overall theory.

The Notion of Resistance

We start with the notion of resistance. Beginning with Freud, keen observers of human behavior have noticed that people often seem to resist letting go of the attitudes and emotions that make them miserable. They avoid the very thing that presumably would help them most by relieving the emotional pain they are suffering. What's more, this resistance bears all the signs of being planned and carried out intentionally—with the single exception that the sufferer seems unaware of planning and carrying it out intentionally. This strategic aspect of many forms of emotional suffering became the hallmark first of the cases Freud treated and then of much of what we have come to know as psychopathology; indeed, his and many later theories are constructed precisely in order to explain why individuals would ever engage in such a strategy.

But that explanation has been elusive. How is it possible for us to adopt an offense-taking and accusing attitude, whereby we feel miserable, without knowing that we are doing so? And if we know this is what we are doing, how can we take our attitude seriously? To engage in emotional behavior on purpose at most amounts to play-acting—pretending to be suffering; it is far from actually undergoing and experiencing such suffering.

The answer for Freud and countless others who have come after has been that we manage to hide what we are doing from ourselves by some slick psychological maneuvering—that's how we can suffer intentionally without being aware that this is what we are doing. But that solution has seemed to many only to answer a problem with another problem: wouldn't this hiding of what we are doing from ourselves make the strategic resistance impossible? Wouldn't we have to know the truth very exactly, as one of Freud's critics pointed out, in order to hide it from ourselves so carefully?

The mainstream answer to this question is that although we have no conscious awareness of what we resist, we are keenly aware of it 'on another level'; we plan and carry out our strategy 'unconsciously'. This is Freud's legacy.

But such an account is unnecessary. This 'solution', which bifurcates mental life into conscious and unconscious realms, is fraught with well-known conceptual problems, it simply does not work. Fortunately we do not need it. An alternative explanation of resistance can be found that has none of its liabilities. By this explanation, which forms part of the core of Warner's work, our strategic resistance to letting go of our offense-taking and accusing attitudes does not depend on our having any awareness of our own mental operations. It completely avoids this mistake.

Attitude and Judgment

A first step toward understanding this new explanation comes with noticing the judgmental character of many emotions we experience.

All offense-taking emotions and attitudes (Warner uses the broad term 'attitudes' to include both) express judgments. To take offense—whether in the form of anger, resentment, hatred, envy, humiliation, etc.—is to express a judgment about the cause of the offense. To be angry, for example, is to make a judgment about the object of our anger; it is to see whomever we are angry with as doing us wrong or as treating us unfairly. The judgments expressed in offense-taking attitudes are accusing judgments.

To accuse others by means of an offense-taking attitude is to make a presentation of oneself. In resenting someone for treating us unfairly, for example, we are also presenting ourselves as being harmed or upset by that treatment. We insist that those we are accusing is causing the agitated state we are in, and that we ourselves are being victimized by them. By our self-presentation we make the claim that they are responsible for what we are suffering and that we bear no responsibility for it.

Thus we present ourselves as passive in our offense-taking/accusing attitudes. We present ourselves as 'only responding to the circumstances', as 'only reacting to what is being done to us'.

Dishonesty

This presentation of ourselves is necessarily false. Precisely because an offense-taking attitude is a self-presentation, it is not what it pretends itself to be. It is not a passive response to the circumstances because it is an active presentation of itself as being a mere response.

This means that accusing attitudes are intrinsically, inescapably dishonest. Each is an active presentation of itself as passive rather than active. (We might say: it is a presentation whose presentation consists precisely in denying that it is a presentation.) To present ourselves as passive and not responsible as we do when maintaining an offense-taking, accusing attitude is to present ourselves falsely.

But if it is true that such attitudes are dishonest, then why we don't we recognize this fact when we are having them? Why are we unable to admit our dishonesty frankly, admit that we are 'up to something' in maintaining this attitude or emotion? We might want to answer that embarrassment explains why we do not admit it to others, but even if true that answer still leaves us with the question why we are not willing to admit it to ourselves. Why do we instead steadfastly believe the false presentation we make of ourselves?

Self-deception

Even though the judgment that is part of an offense-taking, accusing attitude or emotion is false, it is impossible to have that attitude or emotion without believing the judgment to be true. Because the attitude is that judgment, to have the attitude is to be making and believing that judgment. Furthermore, as long as we continue to have that attitude we will be continuing to believe that judgment; so when by our offense-taking attitude or emotion we accuse another, (1) our accusation is necessarily false, and, (2) just as necessarily, we believe it. To adopt such an offense-taking, accusing attitude or emotion is to deceive ourselves.

Self-deception of this kind consists of our having an attitude or emotion the falsity of which we cannot possibly discern. In its nature, such an attitude is a self-deception. Just because it accuses others of causing it, we cannot, in having such an attitude see that we and not those we are accusing are responsible for it.

What Warner's argument shows so far is that an offense-taking, accusing attitude is a lie and that while we have such an attitude we cannot see that it is a lie.

But by itself this is not enough to explain resistance. It explains why an accusing attitude is a self-deception, but it doesn't explain why we continue in self-deception. What prevents us from simply giving up the lie—giving up our accusing attitude—and admitting the truth?

Self-deception as Experience

Just because our false judgment against others and for ourselves is part of an accusing attitude or emotion, we actually experience ourselves as being offended or misused or taken advantage of when we make this judgment. We actually feel humiliated by or angry with or resentful toward those we are accusing. For this reason we cannot doubt that our judgment is true. We cannot seriously call it into question. For to doubt the truth of our judgment against others—to doubt, for example, that they are causing us to feel humiliated—would be to doubt whether we are really *feeling* humiliated. And about that we can have no doubt, because in that very moment we are in fact feeling humiliated.

Moreover, any suggestion that we are not really feeling that way can only be interpreted by us as meaning that we are merely pretending to feel humiliated. But since we know we are not merely pretending, this idea can only strike us as preposterous in the extreme.

Thus the attitude and feelings we have toward others when we accuse them 'prove' to us that our accusation is true. Although illogical, in our accusing mind our anger or resentment or envy *itself* stands as firm evidence that those we are accusing are guilty.

So the reason we can't admit the truth when our attitude or emotion is accusing is that we cannot even see this truth. The only alternative we can see to the judgment that others are responsible for making us feel as we do is the possibility that we don't really *feel* as we do. And this we know is absurd.

It is because our false judgment on the one hand and our attitude or emotion on the other are inseparably connected—one thing described in two different ways—that we cannot fail to be convinced that this judgment is true and to preclude ourselves from entertaining even the possibility that we might be wrong. Self-deception permeates experience.

But we still need to know what accounts for the resistant quality of self-deception. If we 'just know' we are right in our offense-taking, accusing attitudes toward others, then why do we seem to hold those attitudes so insistently? Why do we seem to be resisting something in the way we hold them?

A Self-troubling Act

One of the essential features of any accusing, offense-taking attitude, as we have seen, is its self-presentational character. To have such an attitude or emotion is to present ourselves as being free of responsibility for it, to make an assertion, by our manner if not our words, that we are free of this responsibility. The implications of this truth about offense-taking, self-asserting attitudes and emotions are sweeping.

First of all, such attitudes are inherently negative. They are denials of responsibility. "You are the problem here," when asserted by means of an accusing attitude or emotion, is inseparably linked with the protestation, "I'm *not* the problem here." Though we are capable of purely affirmative attitudes and emotions, such as love, delight, and grief, the varieties of offense-taking are not among them. Self-assertion always consists of a denial.

Second—and this is a further implication—by consisting of a denial, an offense-taking attitude or emotion calls attention to the possibility of its own falsehood. To insist by the way we present ourselves that we are not responsible calls attention to the possibility that we might be responsible after all. Our insistence raises, and calls attention—others' attention and our own—to the very possibility it denies. We raise in our own minds the possibility that we might be responsible for it after all.

Thus our self-presenting act of maintaining an accusing attitude is inherently 'troubled,' agitated, self-disturbing. It is troubled by the upsetting possibility that what it claims might be false, and that in claiming this, the act itself might be fraudulent. An experienced challenge to its own credibility and honesty inheres in the performance of any such attitude or emotion. Anxiety permeates its interior. It constantly raises the possibility of its own fraudulence by denying it.

This possibility—that this challenge to our credibility and honesty might have merit—is what we resist. And it is a possibility raised by our offense-taking attitude itself. That attitude thus creates the very challenge it resists. It troubles itself. Constant self-assertion equals constant anxiety equals constant resistance.

Strangely, the challenge produces this deep anxiety and elicits this resistance even while completely lacking credibility.

We *know* it to be preposterous. In our minds, our experience of feeling offended absolutely validates our judgment. And yet we continue agitated, troubled, disturbed. The explanation for this turns upon the fundamental fact that the accusing attitude or emotion and the judgment made by means of it are one and the same. The idea that we might be wrong has got to be preposterous because we are actually experiencing offended feelings. But at the same time we cannot ignore this challenge as we would some other utterly preposterous accusation because we keep throwing it in our own face as long as we continue to have these feelings.

Third, the possibility that we resist in deceiving our-selves—in having accusing, offense-taking attitudes—is not any sort of truth. It is not what we might believe or acknowledge if only we were not deceiving ourselves. What we resist is a possi-bility created by our accusation, by our denial of it. This means that, contrary to Freudian models, our self-deception is not an avoidance or repression of an awareness we find threatening. It is not an act—a logically impossible act—of intentionally hiding anything from ourselves. We create what we resist by resisting it. Offense-taking is resistant and can never cease to be. The only way to end the self-deception is not to admit a truth resisted, since there is no such truth, *but to cease creating the falsehood resisted.* The only way to end the self-deception is to cease taking offense.

The Totality of Self-deception

In our self-induced self-deception, we cannot see, can-not fathom, the possibility that those we accuse are not guilty and we are not innocent. We have discovered why: it would mean doubting the experience we are having even while having it. The horizon of possibilities that we can entertain while in this condi-tion excludes the truth. All the alternative interpretations of our circumstances available to us are false. We have in effect creat-ed for ourselves a virtual reality, our preoccupation with which keeps us from being able to suspect its inauthenticity and imagine reality itself.

The attitudes which account for much human unhappiness—the feelings in which we take ourselves to be provoked, used, victimized, or in some manner overcome—are resistant to change because of the kinds of attitudes they are. Because they are accusations of others and presentations of ourselves, such attitudes are intrinsically resistant.

What does this intrinsic resistance imply about 'hidden' motivation—about the role of unconscious processes in explaining resistance?

Hidden Motivation and the Unconscious

The falsity of our belief in others' guilt and our own innocence, when we adopt offense-taking, accusing attitudes and emotions, is not some hidden fact of which we are aware 'on some level' but resist. Instead, what we resist is created by and part of our self-deception, and only arises with it. What appears to motivate our defensive and insistent attitude is a function or product of the attitude itself.

This means that the hypothesis of unconscious processes is superfluous. Such processes were invented to supply the motivation for resistance. But resistance can be fully and coherently accounted for without reference to any such 'hidden' processes.

The idea of the unconscious, then, is doubly deficient. It is self-contradictory, hypothesizing motives, supposedly attended to and unknown at the same time, that logically cannot play the part assigned to them. And it is theoretically extraneous: what it wants to explain—self-deceived behavior—can be explained without postulating any hidden process.

The attitudes and emotions by which we make ourselves miserable, then, are intrinsically resistant and intrinsically self-deceptive. Their natural structure is such that we resist changing them even while experiencing the misery they entail. Making ourselves miserable and resisting change are two sides of one coin.

The question now is: Why does anyone ever have such defensive and accusing attitudes in the first place? In what context and for what reason do they arise at all?

The attitudes and emotions by which we make ourselves miserable, then are intrinsically resistant and intrinsically self-deceptive. Their internal structure is such that we resist changing them even while experiencing the misery they entail. Making ourselves miserable and resisting change are two sides of one coin.

The question now is: Why does anyone ever have such defensive and accusing attitudes in the first place? In what context and for what reason do they arise at all?

Self-betrayal

Let us call an act in which we do what we feel to be wrong an act of 'self—betrayal.' In such an act, we go against our own endorsement or assent to the rightness, for us, of a particular course of action. We go against our own fundamental moral commitments. We betray ourselves.

The only way we can carry off this self-betrayal is to do it hypocritically—to do it in a way that makes the wrong we are doing appear right, or at least not wrong. It is to do all we can do, given that we are doing wrong, to make this wrong, this refusal to do right, morally conscientious. Of course we cannot make it conscientious in fact, since it is not. But we can insist by the way we do it that it is morally conscientious. We present ourselves so. Self-betrayal is always concerned to justify itself.

In this assertion of conscientiousness, we acknowledge the sovereignty, for us, of the morality or rectitude that we are refusing to be governed by. In the way we dishonor it, which is by trying to justify ourselves, we honor it. We live a lie.

This self-justifying lie takes the form of an accusation. We blame others in order to shift responsibility for the wrong we are doing away from ourselves. This is how we present ourselves as morally conscientious. In our warped perception, others' blameworthiness excuses us if our acts are less than exemplary ("How can she expect me to be considerate when she acts the way she does?"), and it brings us credit if, despite our belief that we are being mistreated, we nevertheless behave outwardly in the manner of a conscientious person. ("I will treat her considerably even though she doesn't remotely deserve it.") Since in blaming the other person we actually feel offended, as we have seen, we can convince ourselves that *whatever* we do—justified if we give into the provocation we are feeling, and justified if we 'nobly' rise above it.

(The second example is a case of self-betrayal because even there we are failing to do what we are assenting to do—even there we are not really being considerate but are instead displaying our moral superiority through a self-righteous deigning-to-be-considerate.)

The two responses are just variant ways to act upon the accusing attitude or emotion to which the self-betrayal gives rise. In one, we blame another for our failure to do what we, in the very act, are endorsing as right for us to do, and by this means exonerate ourselves. In the other, we 'rise above' the mistreatment we feel sure we are receiving and, in our outward behavior though not in our feelings, do as we feel we ought to do—do 'the best a person can' when feeling so mistreated. Both courses of action are ways of carrying out the basic self-betrayal.

Accusing attitudes and emotions—the psychological conditions in which we self-deceivingly make ourselves miserable—originate in self-betrayal. The ultimate accounting for them is moral or ethical. This explains why in having an accusing attitude or emotion moral or ethical issues dominate our attention: we make excuses, we fault others, and we defend ourselves.

These would not be issues for us if we were at peace with ourselves morally and ethically.

Reality

The picture of the social world as an arena of intrinsically self-seeking and defensive beings—as "a paranormal of allergic egos", in Emmanuel Levinas' description—is a virtual reality, the product of the technology of defense inevitably employed by self-betrayers. Freed from this virtual reality, we would see others and ourselves differently, truthfully. It would be clear to us that their accusations of us and their defense of themselves have nothing whatever to do with us, but only express their own struggle to save themselves in their self-betrayals. Hence we would have no occasion to take offense, no need to accuse them in return. The end of attitudinal and emotional misery comes, and comes only, with renunciation of self-betrayal.

The question that began this introduction to Warner's work was: How and why do we resist changing the very emotions that make us miserable? The answer is, these emotions and attitudes are accusing and inherently dishonest—and for this reason they are intrinsically resistant. They are inherently self—perpetuating because inherently self-deceptive.

The final question was: Why does anyone ever have such attitudes to begin with? The answer is: self—betrayal. When we betray ourselves we generate attitudes by which we blame others and justify ourselves. These accusing attitudes are our self-deceptions. Our unhappiness—the miserable emotions we seem unable to change—arise from our wrong-doings, as efforts to be justified in them.

All of this means that to deceive ourselves in these attitudes, and to resist change, is not to perform a special act of mental subterfuge or concealment, as Freud and his theoretical cousins have thought. It is simply to perform this ordinary act—self-betrayal—whose very properties are self-deceiving and thus self-perpetuating.

As a brief sketch of the central thread of Warner's argument, this treatment obviously omits most of Warner's actual work. Nevertheless, some of its sweeping implications (all of which have been explored by Warner, and some of which appear in the accompanying essays) should be apparent.

For one thing, a corollary of this argument is the centrality of moral experience in understanding all of human conduct. Far from being just one dimension of human personality, moral experience seems instead to be the very ground of human personality.

Second, to be in self-betrayal is not to modify our experience in peripheral ways; it is to enter a whole new way of being, and to inhabit a virtual reality in which others are to be resented and we ourselves freed form responsibility. It is to distort our experience, both of ourselves and others, in a radical and unhappy manner.

Third, we can no longer think of social interaction in the familiar ways we are accustomed to; to the extent we are self-deceiving, we do not act independently of one another. We take whatever others may be doing as our excuse for our accusing treatment of them, and thereby give them excuse for their mistreatment of us. Together we create and reinforce for one another the self-deceived reality in which we each feel unfairly treated, and each are convinced we alone are completely justified.

Fourth, understanding self-betrayal and the nature of the self-deception it generates alters our understanding of the very idea of understanding; what we believe about ourselves and others is the product of our moral or ethical responses. We cannot control our social cognitions cognitively; we can only control them morally.

Fifth, reality differs profoundly from what we believe when we are entrapped in offense-taking attitudes or emotions.

We have glimpses of this in our best moments of having been deluded about the possibility of this reality when we betray ourselves. Freedom from self-betrayal means inhabiting reality. Sixth, the view of human nature embodied in Warner's work transforms our understanding of personal and social change. It explains (a) why genuine change—change in one's very way of being—is possible at all, (b) what its structure is when it occurs, and (c) how the conditions for such change can (and cannot) be deliberately pursued.

I

ANGER AND SIMILAR
DELUSIONS[1]

We are in the midst of a reassess-
ment, in several disciplines, of long standing assumptions about
emotion. The most vigorous new work seems to be concen-
trating not so much on the cognitive aspect of many emotions,
which is well enough recognized by now, but the active, purpo-
sive and indeed strategic aspects; this work regards emotions as
conduct—as manoeuvres or 'moves' in largely institutionalized

1 An earlier version of this paper was presented to the Utah Academy of Arts and Sciences, May, 1984. Arthur King,
Dennis Packard, Merlin Myers, Bernard Harrison, Eddy Zemach and Rom Harré have made suggestions that I have
made use of, not necessarily as they might have wished. The influence of Harré, in the final draft, and of King are
generally too pervasive to document specifically.

social interactions involving clusters of people at once. Thus patterns of emotion, like rhetorical phenomena, are culturally indigenous. Their use is governed by expectations implicit in the moral order of the society and period in which they are to be found, expectations that pertain to such matters as rights, status, and appropriateness. Among a given people, particular kinds of emotion arise, flourish, and then pass into extinction, and at every stage are subject to diffusion, export, and adaptation.[2]

In spite of increasing evidence for this 'social constructionist' view of emotion, its truth is far from obvious. On the contrary, in having an emotion—when, for example, we are ashamed, fearful, depressed, jealous, proud, or head over heels in love—what we think is going on with us is a far cry from anything that can be called conduct. We regard our emotion as a condition provoked or aroused in us—"You are making me angry"—or as a condition that has befallen us—"I think it's her son's rebelliousness that's saddened her so profoundly." The cases that interest me most are the kind exemplified by anger, for in being angry a person is making a judgment that the object of her anger (whatever or whomever it is she is angry with) and not she herself, is responsible for her anger. So if it is true that in being angry she is engaging in a form of conduct, it is a conduct in and by which she maintains that she is not doing so at all, but is passive. Angry people are systematically in error in their beliefs about how things are with them.

I am interested not solely in anger, but in all emotions that have this property: when we are experiencing the emotion, we are certain we are being caused to have it. For convenience I shall simply treat one of these emotions, *anger,* as exemplary. It should not be difficult for the reader to generalize my conclusions to other emotions possessing the required property, such as contempt, (psychological) irritation, hate, embarrassment,

2 A good synoptic discussion and introduction to the literature on these subjects is found in Rom Harré, *Personal Being* (Oxford: Basil Blackwell, 1983). See especially J. Labini and M. Silver, *Moralities of Everyday Life* (Oxford: Oxford University Press, 1982), and Carol Tavris, *Anger: The Misunderstood Emotion* (New York: Simon and Schuster, 1982).

dread, jealousy, self-pity, and boredom, and many, but not all, instances of what we call indignation, anxiety, guilt, and indifference.

Now on the social constructionist view, systematically pursued or maintained conduct, including emotions, are embedded in complex social practices involving other people, whose responses are both anticipated and utilized. For this reason, the judgments in which particular avowals on expressions of emotion consist cannot be merely mistaken. Insofar as the social practices that embed them are concerned, they are manoeuvres, stratagems, etc. The angry person's misunderstanding of herself is something she systematically sustains in a kind of morbid cooperation with others. It is not enough to say she is deceived. She is self-deceived: and, generally speaking, the others abet her self-deception.

How to account for the self-deception of angry people and people experiencing relevantly similar emotions is the problem of this paper. It is a problem worthy of attention because the standard kind of account makes reference to psychical acts or processes of which the person is not aware—acts or processes that Freud called unconscious. On this view, the stratagems or manoeuvres in which self-deceiving conduct consists operate on a level or in a stratum unavailable to introspection: 'the unconscious'. There are two general difficulties with the notion of the unconscious. As is well known, it is internally inconsistent; I will talk about this difficulty in due course. But more to the point of this paper, as an explanation of social behaviour, the unconscious is radical individualistic rather than social. (In Freud, the mentation that makes the expression of emotion an instance of conduct rather than a mechanical response is wholly internal; and the fact that this mentation is socially influenced does not make it less so.) Indeed, the inconsistency of the concept of the unconscious can be traced precisely to the individualism of it (though showing why this is so lies beyond this paper). The problem before us, then, is to account for the sort of self-deception in which anger and similar emotions consist without reference to internal, unconscious processes, but instead by reference to the corporate social episodes of which such emotions are a part.

To develop an account of this sort, I shall:

1. Explore the self-deception that accompanies anger and similar emotions;

2. Examine their 'strategic' aspects, by which they coordinate themselves with the strategies of others in patterned social episodes; and

3. Explain how the agents engaged in these emotions deceive themselves as to the character of what they are doing, and construct this explanation without reference to unconscious stratagems or processes.

My position will be that we deceive ourselves by adopting a self-deceiving rhetoric of moral conscientiousness and excuse—the rhetoric includes our avowals of emotion—and, by this means, presenting ourselves as morally justified. Such self-presentation is contrary to what a straightforward outsider can plainly observe of what we are doing. We make ourselves out to be acting conscientiously, whereas others can tell that, rather than acting conscientiously, we are merely making themselves out to be doing so, which is a dissembling rather than a conscientious thing to do.

Before undertaking the three tasks I have outlined, it will be useful if I speak a bit more precisely about the theses I will defend.

To say that anger possesses the property I mentioned above—that the angry person believes she is being caused to be angry—is to say that she believes herself to be responding to a threat provided wholly independent of her will. It is this threat she thinks is causing her to be angry. She believes herself a victim: whatever she is doing is undertaken only in her own defence. From an observer's point of view, we will want to grant that she may be wrong in this prototheory of the genesis of her anger (though this is something *she* cannot concede without thereby ceasing to be angry). One way to capture this more tentative view is to say the anger is *defensive*; we would mean by this that the agent believes it an effect of an independent provocation, and we would take no position on whether her belief is true.

The received doctrine that we are not responsible for being angry actually consists of two erroneous doctrines, very closely related to each other. One of these doctrines amounts to a semi sympathetic interpretation of the agent's view of her own anger. This interpretation allows that the agent may be mistaken in her judgment that she is caused to be angry by circumstances beyond her control. Yet it assumes that the judgment is sincere and that she is responding straightforwardly to these circumstances as she (perhaps erroneously) sees them. This might be called the *doctrine of sincerity or straightforwardness*. The second doctrine follows from the first: though the angry judgment may be mistaken about how it is being caused, it is not also mistaken about *whether* it is caused, and this on account of its sincerity. At the very least, it is caused by the belief the angry person has (sincerely held if false) about how it is being caused, or by the psychological state of having this belief, or by the onset of this belief. This doctrine, which is also a sympathetic interpretation of the sincerity doctrine, I shall call *the causal view of anger*.

Before sketching out my line of attack against these two doctrines, I want to indicate briefly the dependency of the causal view of anger upon a hard edged distinction between judgment and feeling, or cognition and affect. (The untenability of this distinction in this context will become a point of issue later on.) This distinction is the means by which the causal view grants the corrigibility of the angry individual's view of her anger without altogether abandoning the idea that anger is caused. The self-explanatory character of anger is assigned to a judgment component of the emotion—it is this judgment that is corrigible—which is accordingly separated from a feeling component.

That this is necessary for the causal view is made clear by considering how the causalist would respond to the following objection: "Suppose that A, to this point angry at B, were to abandon her belief that B had done what (up to now) she has supposed has been angering her. If this happened, her anger would cease. This argues against the causal view and for the *identity* of anger and the judgment it involves. In a clear case of causality, if a person at first believed a safety razor caused the cut on her arm, and then changed her mind when she discovered fresh blood on the shower door, the cut would not disappear. But when there is this sort of change of mind about the cause of one's anger, the anger ceases. How then can anger be contingent upon anything external, as the angry person believes it is?" To this objection the advocate of the causal view would have to respond as follows: The fact that A's anger ceases if her judgment changes can be accounted for causally. The kind of causality her anger imputes is not a direct causality. Her judgment against B respecting whatever he is doing to anger her is separate from, and prior to, her angry feelings, and it is this judgment, not B's act itself, that directly causes the feeling. The production of the feeling is, as they say, cognitively mediated. In the event that the judgment is correct, the object might be said by some to be the cause A believes it is, by way of her perception and otherwise not, or the psychological state of making the judgment might be said to be the cause, or the onset of this state. In summary: the causal view of anger must account for the corrigibility of anger, and the way it can do this without abandoning the causality doctrine is by separating judgment from feeling and regarding the judgment, but not the feeling, as corrigible. A might say, "I was hurt. If you had said what I thought you said, you would have been responsible for what I've gone through. I can see now that it was all a tragic misunderstanding on my part."

This response to the objection leaves intact the core conviction of the angry individual, namely, that she is not responsible for her anger. That is why I said the causal view is semi sympathetic to that conviction. We can now isolate precisely the irreducible core of the causal view must maintain: the angry individual is not responsible for her angry *feelings*. She might under certain circumstances admit some responsibility for her judgment, e.g. "I'm sorry; I should have listened to you more carefully." But in no case will she admit responsibility for the feelings, since in her mind they are not the sort of thing that she could be responsible for. Respecting her feelings, she believes herself a pure patient. And in this belief she is not alone; the idea that we are not responsible for our defensive feelings is an almost unassailed dogma of our culture.

Two Interlocking Theses

A major difficulty with the causal view is that, as an interpretation of anger's defensiveness, it is incompatible with an interpretation of that defensiveness implicit in common usage. In other words, there are socially observable properties of angry conduct in the absence of which we would never ascribe anger, yet which are inexplicable if the causal view were true, and anger were straight-forwardly defensive. The interpretation that alone can explain these properties, rival to the causal view, is that anger is *resistant*, or in other words, motivated by ulterior considerations respecting others rather than straightforwardly caused. On this interpretation, the angry person's view that her anger is an effect of causes is not sincere; it is a *self-deception*. The straightforwardness doctrine is false. I will show how, in anger, we systematically distort both our understanding of the anger itself and what it is 'about'. The emotions of which anger is representative are so common in almost everyone's life that, because of them, most of us most of the time systematically misunderstand both ourselves and others.

This *thesis of self-deception* implies that the angry individual is not simply wrong about what, beyond her control, is responsible for her anger, but about whether *anything* beyond her control is responsible for it. This means that the causal view also is false. My denial of the causal view is an affirmation of the agent's responsibility for her anger; I'll call it the *thesis of agency*. This agency thesis does not, so far as I can see, reciprocally entail the thesis of self-deception. As the argument of this paper is for the resistance, i.e. the self-deception, of anger, which is the stronger of the two theses, the argument will if successful hit both of my targets, and otherwise neither.

What is at stake in trying to establish the self-deception thesis, and by means of this the responsibility thesis, is the interpretation of anger's defensiveness. In showing that the defensiveness consists in resistance, which is a public and social act rather than a private one, I shall keep a constant eye upon the self-deception literature. For it will turn out that the essentially social account I give of the self-deceptiveness of anger will constitute a full-blown account of self-deception that at once accommodates all the observable aspects of self-deceived conduct and is free of the well known conceptual debilities that have afflicted previous theories.

THE CASUAL VIEW OF ANGER

Accusation and Victimhood

There are two mutually entailing aspects of anger's defensiveness. The first is its accusatory quality. To an angry individual her anger seems to be the effect, in her, of someone else's conduct. "I resent her for saying I'm not qualified for the job." "Of course I'm bitter. He up and dies without leaving me enough to pay the mortgage." In her view, another person(s) is maliciously (or inconsiderately) and unfairly transgressing her rights or abusing her interest or violating her dignity, and the result is her self-protective, accusing emotion. She sees this other person as dealing unfairly (a question of rights) with her to her disadvantage (a question of interests), and therefore as morally responsible for the emotion.

Suppose that one individual heretofore angry at another were suddenly to concede that the other is not responsible for her anger. This concession would constitute a giving up of that anger. Were we not prepared to respond to the concession in this manner, we would be using the term 'anger' in an uncommon sense.[3] For example, imagine that we realize we have profoundly misunderstood the intentions of someone we have been angry with—someone, for instance, who has failed to keep an appointment after we have gone to great inconvenience to meet him. As we wait, increasingly upset, we re-examine our relationship to him. It begins to bother us, perhaps as it never has before, that so much in the past can be seen, on reflection, to manifest his disrespect for us, our time, and our feelings. It bothers us also that we have been so naive as to overlook this repeated thoughtlessness. We are confident that he could have come on time had he wanted to enough, had it been among his priorities, had he not been selfish or insensitive. Then we receive a report that he has been in an accident. Suddenly what was mounting anger ends, and in its place we feel chagrin for having

---

3   This is not the occasion to discuss the epistemological status of remarks such as these on the meaning of a word, but if it were it would address the difficulties of discovering, in any other way than I discovered it, what we mean by 'anger'. And how did I discover it? I discovered (learned) it by becoming a representative member of a community that uses this word, helped by myriad responses to my attempts from other such representatives, until I became one of those in whose verbal conduct, the responses of others to me, and the written and recorded traces of these interactions, that meaning is now reposited. In other words, I became participant in those social forms that Wittgenstein called 'language games', which are institutions of conduct mediated by speech. I would also address the difficulties inherent in establishing 'empirically' how others in this community use the word 'anger' independently of how I use it, when in order to do so I must presume agreement about the meaning of many other closely related words, whose meaning for us would not remain unaltered if we discovered that 'anger' means something different from what we thought.

transgressed against a friend by unjustifiably bringing a charge against him in our hearts, which is to say, by unjustifiably becoming angry at him. We are chagrined because the unjustifiability of the angry charge renders it, in our own eyes, a transgression. Coupled with the chagrin is a sense of relief that we refrained from acting overtly on the anger while it lasted. Though anger has given way to chagrin and relief, it is still as true as it was a few moments before that we have been inconvenienced. The only thing that has changed is our belief, essential to the anger while it lasted, that the other party has transgressed against us and is therefore responsible for what we have been suffering.[4]

Indissociably connected with this accusing quality is a sense in the angry person of being passive, victimized, and helpless. She feels she is a pure patient in the face of forces she cannot control. In the angry person's mind the accused can control some of these, if he but will: and that is precisely why she feels his victim. She does not believe merely that she is acting under duress or coercion. She believes she is not acting at all, but is passive. She not only bears no responsibility for her anger, she could bear none, however emotionally strong, resilient, or self-controlled she might be. It is the very nature of this kind of emotion, as she understands it while having it, that she could not be responsible for it. At the same time, she does not necessarily think the other is the sole cause of her anger. She can freely admit that her own temperament and her history with him are factors that render her vulnerable to him. But she does believe his conduct to be an intrusion into prevailing and otherwise tranquil conditions, and therefore can be blamed for her agitation. The key here is that, as far as she is concerned, the causes and conditions she would identify for her anger are beyond her present control.

---

[4] It is possible to regard angry people as others operating on one 'meta' level or another, relative to those they are angry with. In the example, being justified in our treatment of another consists in our moral assessment of whether the other is justified in his response to us. Our response to him is mediated by our contemplation of his justification relative to the moral order that we have in common. Later, I shall return to these considerations.

The accusation in an angry attitude is directed toward something beyond the attitude itself, whereas the sense of victimhood correlative to that accusation is self-conscious. In anger there is always a sense of being a victim with respect to rights or interests that are felt to be violated; in some cases this takes the form of self-pity. The accusation and the sense of being victimized are correlative because seeing another as provoking oneself is to feel provoked. Taken as a unit, this accusing/victimized attitude—this belief that the anger is a defence—is what we might call 'the angry view of anger.' The angry person incessantly puts forward an explanation of her anger by imputing responsibility for it elsewhere. She is essentially self-conscious, which is to say, self-regarding about whatever losses of rights, privileges, or interests she feels she is suffering. She feels she is not the sort of person who deserves being treated in this way.

Illustration of Anger's Self-conscious, Self-explanatory Character

Notice in the following completely banal episode, in which two people are angry at each other, how this quality is progressively revealed as each party feels increasingly challenged about the legitimacy of his or her position.

Brent. It's ten minutes to eight, Alison, and . . .

Alison. I know, don't tell me, I haven't even showered yet. Obviously this is one party you want to go to or you wouldn't care about being late.

Brent. Since we're seeing my friends, you're not going to hurry, is that it?

Alison. Have I been standing around? After I got home from work I fed Sarah and got her ready for bed and you've only taken care of yourself.

Brent. If you really cared you could have been ready on time.

Alison. Look, Mister, I've been working most of the

day and then cleaned up the kitchen and got a babysitter just so we could go.

Brent. You think you're the only one who works around here. I come home early three days a week so you can take classes after you get off work, and I passed up a good promotion because you didn't want to live in Placerville, and all you can think of is how much you do and how little I do.

Alison. You let me off duty for a few hours and you think you've made a big sacrifice. You're off duty just about all the time! What's the matter? Does it cut into your freedom when I get to go out for an hour?

Brent. So it's all my fault, is it? I'm always the one who causes our problems.

Alison. Everything I said was true.

Brent. If you're convinced I'm so selfish, how can you stand me? Why don't you just leave?

Alison. Here we go. The Great Victim rides again.

Brent. To hear you tell it, I'm always the one who's in the wrong.

Alison. I never said that. Remember, you were the one who blamed me first.

Brent. I don't even feel like going to the party anymore.

Alison. I can't believe it. You need help. You're really sick.

Variant Anger Styles

A subcultural designation for the style of this exchange between Alison and Brent might be "American assertive." In other cultures, classes, or subcultures, the style of offense taking might well be different from theirs. In some such groups, for example, anger is typically even more volatile and sometimes, though not in all cases, less calculated and sinister and/or less durable (e.g. Tikopians, youthful Nuer males, Neapolitans). On the other end of a particular dimension, there are cultures and classes within cultures in which open altercation would be unthinkable or uncouth; in these, the accusation of another tends more pronouncedly to be a matter of making clear one's own victimized status. Some varied examples of this are ritualized clamour (Australian aborigines), accusing the object of one's anger of bewitching one (Tiv, Nyakyusa, Azande), histrionic suicide (Trobiander), and chilly silence (upper class British). In some cultures the offender is treated with an intensified 'respectfulness' expressed by an increased formality of vocabulary and intonation (Korean). These matters are extensively treated in the literature of social and psychological anthropology.

What is common to these diverse cases is that the angry individual's offended status, and thereby his accusation, is unmistakably communicated by means of conventional and sometimes even ritual conduct that in its own way is just as defensive and, yes, self-assertive as the emotions of Brent and Alison during their falling-out.[5] To point out this commonality is to make no anthropological claim about the emotions characteristic of any peoples. Strictly speaking, it would be irrelevant to my thesis if it happened that some, many, or even all known cultures lacked the defensive emotions I have defined. (Among the Nez Perce multiple families lived in the same house for generations without trouble, and it is said that the 24 Tasadays had in their language no word for anger or anything resembling it.) My interest is only in showing why any emotions possessing the ac-

---

5 Harré has pointed out to me that, in some cases, the conduct may be an 'amplification' of the offended status, as with the Australian aborigine and the Trobriander, and in other cases, like the increasing deference of the Korean, a 'minimization' of it. I put these qualifications in scare quotes because they themselves are part of the anger. They are part of the self-justifying manoeuvre that is taking place. For example, the Koreans' deference can be thought of as a move in a metagame, by which he can punish more effectively by displaying himself as morally superior to those at whom his anger is directed.

cusing, self-victimizing properties I have specified cannot but be self-deceptions, whether and wherever these emotions happen to be manifest. In this paper I shall track the example of Brent and Alison through, with the proviso that a culturally different sort of accusing and self-victimizing emotion could have been chosen to illustrate my points.

The Contrast of Defensive Emotions and Other Kinds

It is worth noting also that although the expressions of anger between Alison and Brent are defensive, this is not true of everything we would be willing to call anger. It is possible, for example, that Jesus' castigation of the money changers in the temple was not an accusation to the effect that those he drove before him were responsible for how he felt toward them. It is possible, in other words, that his attitude was more other-concerned, or perhaps even concerned for a principle, than self-concerned. It is possible, in other words, that it was more like love or integrity than hostility, even though appropriately called 'anger'. I do not know whether this usage would be metaphorical or extended. One can chastise or reprimand—and be properly said to be angry—without feeling a victim.

These remarks suggest that to talk of accusing emotions like anger is to classify emotions in a manner different from their classification in the natural languages with which I am familiar. There may be emotions that impute causality but not malice or inconsiderateness to their objects, e.g. arousals such as instinctive fear of immediate physical threat. Such an arousal is not what I have been calling a defensive emotion. It seems certain also that some emotions impute no external causality at all, e.g. love, grief, and joy. The lover who insists, "I can't help loving you," or "You made me love you," is an infrequent and, I think, marginal case. To love art, a child, one's companion of many years, gardening, or silence, it is not necessary, definitely not usual, and perhaps even abnormal to insist by one's attitude that what one loves is making one love it. Defensive emotions, then, are but one kind of emotion, instances of which are distributed among the various groupings of emotions that we commonly make.

PROBLEMS WITH THE CASUAL VIEW

Inapplicability of the Judgment/Feeling Distinction

The judgment/feeling dichotomy, required if the causal view is to account for the corrigibility of anger, breaks down when the attempt is made systematically to understand anger in terms of it. We have seen already that the judgment embedded in anger is not simply about the anger-object, but about the angry individual himself. What A is doing that is relevant to his being angry is seen by B not simply as conduct wholly external, but as conduct *just insofar as it affects him.* An unselfconscious judgment, or even an earnest assertion, *entirely* about another would be independent of anger and therefore not be the sort of accusation that anger makes. The accusation that is anger, on the other hand, being explicitly or implicitly self-referential ("Alison, you are being unfair to me"), *cannot* be independent of the experience of anger. If the content of that judgment is that one is being psychologically or emotionally violated, it cannot be a sincerely made judgment without being also a feeling or experience of being violated (which the angry person takes himself to be). (This means that anger of the kind we are studying is not concerned wholly with another's deviation from a principle, but with violation of personal rights—of rights that constitute him the kind of person one is. The offense is experienced as a deep violation of what one is as a person.) Thus, what B thinks is his perception of A's offensive conduct can be *nothing other than* B's taking offense. There is no perception of offensiveness that is not also a taking of offense.

Someone might object that the perception and the feeling might be separate yet always concomitant. I consider this objection a concession that there are no good grounds, beyond a need to defend the causal view, for dividing anger into two components, a cognitive one and an affective one, judgment and feeling. These are abstractions drawn for some localized purpose from a total conduct in a total social situation engaging the organism totally, and in the present context are profoundly misleading.

So agentively speaking, B's anger is not what the causal view of his anger implies it is, namely, a complex reaction consisting of several sequential moments, including an evaluative judgment and a subsequent affective arousal. It is not first a perception of offensiveness followed by a taking of offense. It is, instead, one thing, a totality, a being-offended-at-a-perceived-offense. Our taking offense does not depend upon the other's offensiveness; it is (our perception of) his offensiveness. Our anger does not depend upon the other's malice (or callousness); it is (our perception of) his malice insofar as that malice has any power to anger us. Our anger-judgments concern both our adversaries and ourselves at once; it is not merely that we are blameless *because* they are blameworthy, but we are blameless *in* their blameworthiness. Our exoneration is their culpability. In anger, accusation equals self-justification.

In passing we should note that from this point of view we can readily understand the perhaps infrequent but undeniable cases in which we perceive that another's angry act is maliciously intended toward us, and yet we are not reciprocally angry but compassionate. A compassionate perception of malice is not a taking of offense, and as *perception* differs from one that is. Malice can be perceived, offensiveness against one's person cannot. This is because offensiveness is inextricably connected with the perceiver's sense of being violated in his personal rights, which sense involves a self-justifying appeal by the perceiver to a system of moral principles, principles with which he might or might not be concerned on this particular occasion. It is more accurate, therefore, to speak of taking offense than of being offended. At the same time, it is possible for one person, A, without taking personal offense, to perceive another, B, to be violating—i.e., offending against—the system of principles that constitutes him a person. For A to perceive this is not for her to see B offending or violating her personally, but instead undermining himself. One cannot be disenfranchised from the moral order by another, but only by oneself; hence, perceiving another in this way can be an accurate judgment, whereas taking offense cannot. Such cases tend to be ignored by people who hold the causal view of anger, and when they don't ignore them they tend in an *ad hoc* manner to adduce factors such as traits, dispositions, and moods in order to account for them causally.

In a Causal View, Reciprocal Anger is Impossible

Unexamined, the casual view may seem to accord with our intuitions well enough but in fact has counter-intuitive implications. In this section I shall give examples of such implications.

Angry people assume that the individual(s) they are angry at can be reciprocally angry at them. But insofar as they are angry, they do not and cannot really believe this. In his anger at A, B believes that A is to be blamed—is morally responsible for—his anger, and therefore that A could desist from her offensive attitude toward him if she wished. This makes that attitude different in kind from *his* anger, since he is certain that, given the provocation, *he* can't desist. If he were to suppose otherwise if he were to concede that she is angry in the same sense in which he is angry he would be conceding that she is exactly as free of responsibility for her anger as he believes he is for his, and therefore that she is not malicious and not morally responsible for his anger. This concession would constitute a giving up of his anger. In his anger he can't believe she is angry in the same sense in which he is angry.

Someone might say B could believe himself mistaken in his judgment against A: but though it is true that he might be mistaken, if he *believed* himself mistaken he would no longer be angry.   He can allow that (he is mistaken and) she is really angry only if he is not angry.   This is another of the counter-intuitive implications. (An angry person might say that the individual at whom he is angry is reciprocally angry at him. "Boy, is she ever angry at me!" But this does not mean that he believes she is angry in the same sense in which he is, i.e. justified in being angry.   It means that she is accusing, not that she is legitimately self-protective.) It might also be objected that in being angry B can allow that A is angry *if* he is willing also to allow that she is mistaken in *her* judgment that *he* is maliciously feigning anger. But though he might well allow that she is mistaken, he would in doing so be conceding that she is not responsible for her anger, and this concession would be tantamount to his not being angry.

So under no circumstance can B or any other person consistently believe that two people can be angry with each other if he is one of these people: as far as he is concerned, the other person, the anger-object, can be angry only if he himself is not angry.   And if he allows that she, the anger-object, *is* angry, he must believe her mistaken in her judgment about him and hence not be angry with her.   Nor can anyone holding the causal view of anger consistently believe that any two people can be angry with each other unless he believes that each is mistaken about the other: If A is really angry then, if B is angry, A is mistaken about B, and the same is true of B.

It only compounds my case to realize that part of what B finds offensive may be his sense that A is capable of holding this very view about him: that he can't be angry because she is. Or, even further, that A may be holding that *he* has this view and is excusing himself by means of it, saying in his heart that *she* can't be angry because *he* is.   There is no end to this kind of self-consciousness—or, I should say, this consciousness of 'what we must be doing together'—and no end to the even higher-level offendedness it can induce in the other.[6] The offensiveness of these anticipations of the other's metaperspective on the situation consists, I think, in a sense that it is a deep violation of one's own rights of autonomy and privacy. This goes some way toward explaining why in altercation with intimates we can feel outraged and indeed ravaged to the core of what we are.

Anger's Resistance

The problems concerning the reciprocity of anger seem minor when compared with the inability of the causal view to account for the aspect of anger which I will call its *resistance*. Resistance is an accompaniment of being angry that cannot be reconciled with the causal interpretation of the angry person's defensiveness. It is a rival interpretation of that defensiveness. I want to mention three different, closely related descriptions of the angry person's resistance. These will at first seem unrelated to the familiar, highly individualistic notion of resistance. There is a relationship, however, and I will point it out in the next section.

First: if it were true, as the causal view maintains, that anger is a sincere and straightforward self-explanatory judgment (whether correct or mistaken) to the effect that it is a defence against threat, the behaviour of angry people would be strikingly different from what it is. A threatened person tries to flee from or to terminate the threat. But characteristically an angry person does not behave in either of these ways. Instead he seems to cling to the threat, to make use of it, even to provoke it sometimes, for example, by picking a fight out of the blue, by obsessively brooding over his wounded condition, by overstating his

6 Harré pointed out to me the relevance of these considerations to the opportunities for and limits of reciprocity in angry interactions. For an account of these 'metagames' see R. D. Laing's Sartrian description of interactions as essentially political (especially *Knots*, New York: Vintage Books, 1972) and Harré's account of traps in *Social Being* (Oxford: Basil Blackwell, 1979), especially pp. 212 13.

case in a manner that aggravates the other party, or by fuelling up the quarrel if the other shows signs of letting it die. He may demand satisfaction but typically won't be satisfied. If the other leaves or even dies, he will, if he remains angry, tenaciously carry his grievance with him in his imagination.

A.   I can't take this carping, snivelling attitude of yours any more.

B.   Well then, leave. No one's forcing you to stay.

A.   You think this marriage is holding you back in your career, don't you?

B.   I never said that.

A.   But you think it, don't you? Don't you?

B.   Talking with you doesn't do any good. Let's just forget the whole thing, OK?

A.   Oh, so you're not going to talk it out, huh? What's wrong? Afraid of the truth?

If A were merely defensive and not resistant (whether or not an external threat actually existed), she would not insist upon an interpretation of B's conduct that is unfavourable to her. The behaviour of the angry person resists the demise of its provocation; it refuses to let its provocation die. In a non psychoanalytic sense this can also be called its obsessiveness or compulsivity. Though from A's point of view she is merely defending herself against an external threat, whose victim she feels, from another perspective we can see that she is resistant to the loss of that threat, i.e. obsessive about keeping it alive.

B.   Forget it, will you?

A.   Why should I forget it?

B.   Just get off my back.

A.   How would you feel if I accused you of wrecking *my* career?

The causal view cannot tell us why A resists letting go of the threat she believes B presents. In other words, it cannot explain why what she calls a threat is, for her, an offense, a provocation. As we have seen, the threat itself or even the perception of threat, whether accurate or not, does not explain this. This is because in the causal order the threat is unconnected with the system of rights to which she may or may not be making a self-justifying appeal at the moment. The offense, the provocation, as I have already pointed out, is an event in the moral order, not the causal one.

The second way to describe anger's resistance is as follows. The focus of debate between angry people, either spoken or silent, is almost always upon one issue: Whose accusation is right? We might suppose that this issue could take one of two forms: (a) whether one or the other actually did, or meant to do, what one is accused of doing, and (b) whether one's doing it (or meaning to do it) was sufficient to anger one's accuser. But it cannot take the second form; from the angry person's point of view there can be no debate about the sufficiency of the provocation to provoke. Once it is seen as a provocation, the issue for him is settled.

> B.   What I said was no cause to fly into a rage and attack me.
>
> A.   I suppose you'd like it if I said that to you.

It is settled because, as we see here in the case of A, she actually has her angry feelings. If B is acting as she thinks he is, then in her mind there is no possibility that he is not causing her to feel offended because she is offended, and at him. The only question for debate is whether one or the other did what he or she is accused of doing, i.e., whether the accusing judgment is true or false.

But in spite of this fact, seldom is either of them willing

seriously to consider the possibility of being mistaken in this judgment. Instead, this possibility is systematically resisted. If the causal view were sound, one would expect the protestations each makes of his or her own innocence to be considered by the other. Why not consider this possible way out of a miserable situation? The causal view provides no answer to this question. Indeed, except in infrequent cases, these protestations only infuriate the other more.

> A.   Look, I haven't said a single thing that's unfair to you.
>
> B.   Oh no, you're never in the wrong, are you? You're even too good to live with.

This is but another version of anger's resistance to its own dissolution. On the causal view of anger, there is no accounting for this no reason why the angry person would not be relieved to discover his anger judgment mistaken.

Here is the third description of anger's resistance. We have seen that, so long as B is angry, he cannot understand A to be genuinely angry. Instead he is sure that her accusations of him, and her protestations of doing her best to control herself in the face of his onslaught, are fraudulent. She cannot really have the anger-feelings she says she has. She is cynically using him; she is feigning. This assessment is in fact an aspect of his angry accusation of her. And for her part she senses this accusation, and insofar as she does she feels accused of feigning.[7] But she is in an unassailable position to know that she has her anger-feelings and is not merely pretending. Hence, since she knows her feelings are real, the charge that B makes against her, that she is not legitimately self-protective, that she is to some extent feigning, is preposterous. Yet she does not treat this charge

---

7 Later we are going to see that whether or not he is actually angry and accusing her in this manner—or indeed even knows of her existence—she feels accused simply in virtue of her anger.

as preposterous. She does not laugh at B's accusations or ignore them or even toss them off lightly, as one would the charges of a lunatic or a child. On the contrary, she is obsessive about the need to defend herself against them. She cannot let anything just drop, no matter how inaccurate or absurd. Indeed, it seems that the more outrageous his suggestions are concerning what she is trying to do to him, the more outraged she feels. She will say: "I can't let him get away with that" or "He's attacking my integrity," when what he's saying ought not to matter if it really were preposterous. She might say: "But others might believe him," but she could just as well carry on like this if they were alone together on an island. The persistence of anger in the face of the perceived preposterousness of anger's provocation is a matter so curious that contemplation of it ought to throw almost all previous theorizing about defensive/resistant emotions into confusion. It is the aspect of anger that is least compatible with the individualistically oriented causal view.

THE AGENTIVE VIEW OF ANGER

We have seen that the viewpoint from which the resistance of anger can be recognized and its self-deceptive character entertained—I call it the agentive view—is one that rejects the idea that the angry person is sincere in her defensiveness. It is a viewpoint from which the agent is seen to be 'up to' something else entirely—something that the agent herself is unable to discover. Agentively speaking, anger is self-deception. It should be clear that I do not mean by this that defensive emotions might be instrumentalities by which people deceive themselves, as when one cannot think clearly because of being "too emotional," e.g. infatuated or upset. I mean that these emotions might themselves be self-deceptions.

Before setting forth the agentive view, I want briefly to indicate, as promised, the relationship between the description of the angry person's resistance I have already given and the standard, individualistic, essentially clinical account of resistance. This clinical account is fraught with conceptual problems so great that it has created widespread scepticism in the past about the very notions of resistance and self-deception. Showing that the agentive view is free of these problems is a crucial part of my argument.

By the standard account, the causal view of anger fails not because it makes a causal judgment concerning its own genesis (which, as we shall see, is the agentive explanation of its failure), but because the causal judgment it makes is false. This account leads straight to the position that the resistant emotion-judgments we are talking about are unconsciously motivated. To see this, observe what happens when we try, as the standard account does, to give a causal alternative to the angry person's self-explanation in order to account for resistance. Since the threat the angry person perceives won't explain her nurturing response to it, there must be some other motivating belief that will explain it. What is this belief? It must be (a) a belief (or at least a suspicion) that the facts are not as favourable to her as she insists, and (b) a belief she is not sensible of having—a hidden agenda underlying her conduct, if you will. Such a belief she must be holding in a special cognitive status or on a special cognitive level to which he has no acknowledgeable access. It is commonplace now to characterize this state of affairs by saying she is motivated unconsciously. Thus we see how a search for a causal explanation of the angry person's resistance inevitably leads to the postulation of unconscious processes.

To add to this appearance of unconscious motivation, the angry individual resists too forcibly any suggestion that her case may not be airtight or that she seems to be contributing to her misery herself. When she manifests such resistance, it appears to observers that somebody has gotten uncomfortably close to the truth—that her preoccupation with the threat she says she is under is really her effort to ascribe responsibility elsewhere for what she is doing, a responsibility she unconsciously knows or suspects is hers. For if she did not in some peculiar manner or on some "level" know or suspect it, we want to ask, why would she ever resist a probe that got too near?

Not merely anger but self-deception in general is standardly conceived to be unconsciously motivated. This unconsciously motivated or 'dynamic' self-deception is a problematic conception. According to this conception: An individual brings it about that she actively disbelieves something that she otherwise knows (believes, suspects) is true. A condition for her bringing this about is that she knows (believes, suspects) it to be true. Without this knowledge she would have no occasion for deceiving herself. (Presumably her motivation is the painful or embarrassing nature of the truth she thus knows.) So she must believe in one sense what she makes herself disbelieve in another. It was to avoid this obvious contradiction that Freud devised and a long line of successors endorsed the notion of unconscious processes: it is consciously that the self-deceiver comes to disbelieve what she believes unconsciously. But this move creates as many conceptual problems as it is designed to avoid, problems that render it completely unacceptable.

The treatment these problems require is too extensive to undertake here. But we can indicate here that one of the troubles with the notion of the unconscious is that it separates the resistant emotion from its motivation. Given the separation, the resistant individual must be thought to be reflecting, in an inner, and insulated dialogue upon what she is doing, and in addition denying or belying it by her responsibility-evading anger. Her self-conscious judgment that she is being victimized is preceded by and is in response to another, unconscious self-conscious judgment she is anxious to belie. So it is the doctrine of the separation of resistance and its motivation that lies at the heart of the 'monodramatic'[8] character of the causal view of anger.

This separation of resistant act from its motivation, though apparently an epitome of common sense, it is simply unsupportable where anger is concerned. For it is but an alternate means of making the distinction, mentioned earlier, between judgment and arousal. Earlier we considered this distinction in regard to the accusatory aspect of anger, and saw that we have reason not to think of that aspect as affect-independent. Now, when the issue is resistance, we are considering the distinction in regard to a supposed self-reflective assessment, and will shortly see that here too we have reason to think this assessment an affect-independent judgment.

Here then is the challenge: to account for resistance without recourse to unconscious processes—without recourse, that is to say, to a motivation for resistance that is separate from the resistance. Whatever it is the angry individual resists, it must be found in her accessible (conscious) experience of the social world she finds herself in. (No trait, pattern, or disposition explanation will do when the task is to explain motivated resistance.)

This sort of motivation for resistance is already implicit in the agentive view of anger. Agentively, an angry attitude is an act, embedded in a social pattern of interactions, that takes itself not to be the act that it is; what the angrily resistant person takes herself to be is straightforward, which is to say, one who is not resistantly taking herself to be straightforward, for that is a resistant and unstraightforward thing to do. Fundamentally, it is her act of self-misconstruing that she is misconstruing. It is not something independent of that act that she is misconstruing; it is not something that could possibly be an object of reflection. Whatever self-monitoring might be going on is a systematic misconstrual of the self-monitoring that is going on. There is no

---

8 Harré term; see his Social Being (Oxford: Basil Blackwell, 1979), Ch. 10.

room, therefore, for a self-reflective act of judgment to inter-vene between what she is doing and her act of belying what she is doing. Instead, what she resists admission of, by what she is doing, is precisely the same act as her resistance. Here, in the agentive view, is the suggestion of a motivation for getting or staying angry—a motivation for self-deception—that is not sep-arate from the act of self-deception itself. In other words, it is a motivation that is not separate from the act that resists admitting this self-same motivation (which resistance takes the form of insisting that it is being provoked).

Search for a Metaphor of Defensive Emotion as Action

Before developing this account of self-deception, it will be helpful to have, for the cognitive aspect of anger, a metaphor that does a better job than *judgment* of capturing the self-con-sciousness or self-referentiality, as well as the purposiveness, of that emotion. One candidate is *self-assertion*. Because it is in-extricable from the feelings of anger, what has been called the judgment component might better be thought of as an act—an expression or avowal—that is *itself* resistant to admitting what it may apprehend, albeit self-deceivingly about itself. The re-sistance can be thought to consist in the contrariwise assertion made by the judgment: "Self-assertion" seems a fitting name for such an act.

We can go further. If anger is a kind of self-assertion, it is not necessarily a linguistic kind of assertion. It is more an assertiveness that may receive no verbal formulation at all, either spoken or silent. Much of the quarrel between Alison and Brent could have been, and no doubt was, carried on by means of offended looks, pouting, or morbid feelings. I do not think it bi-zarre to say that the self-assertion—the avowal of self-justifica-tion—involved is the emotion itself and its behavioural expres-sion. There is nothing about either cognition or conduct that coerces us to think that either judgments or assertions need be explicitly formulated. They need not have a particular "logical form" in order to refer to or represent states of affairs. P. Saffra is said to have broken the hold upon Wittgenstein of the picture theory of propositional meaning by a contemptuous gesture of the hand familiar to Neapolitans; "What is the logical form of that?" he asked.[9] We roll our eyes, purse our lips, fidget, wince, sigh, etc., and in so doing express our views and other people get the message—even when there is no separate inner formulation of those views. The unarticulated informational content of such behaviour is what the current study of paralanguage in psychology is all about.

Yet, in spite of the advantages of self-assertion as a metaphor for the kind of thing anger is, someone might say: "If anger is self-assertion, it must depend upon straightforward perceptions of the situation in which it is attempted, including an apprehension of itself. Even a self-assertion whose nature the asserter cannot appreciate while carrying it out (which is the kind of self-assertion that anger would be) is a representation of itself." In answer to this objection, I can only say that the fact that the metaphor of self-assertion doesn't forestall this 'representational' better metaphor. What might it be?

To answer this question, consider this. Anger seems less an attempt to represent or even insist upon one's being a particular kind of person coping with circumstances and more an attempt (albeit an inherently futile one) to be—to establish, make, or constitute oneself—that way. Anger seems a sort of *self-constitution*. It and the other defensive emotions we are studying are, to use Sartre's phrase, "magical transformations" of oneself and one's world.

But to this idea of self-constitution there are objections that must be met. The most serious objection for my purposes is that if, *per impossibile*, anger were conduct undertaken delib-

9 Norman Malcolm, Ludwig Wittgenstein, A Memoir, (London: Oxford University Press, 1958), p. 69.

erately, it would be a cynical misrepresentation, could not take itself seriously, and therefore could not be anger. Further, when we act we may deliberate about doing so, may forbear from doing so, etc., but these things are not possible with anger. Since for these reasons it appears that anger cannot be action, it must instead be precisely what it takes itself to be, namely, not action at all, but passion.

We must be cautious about objections like this, which during my earliest thoughts about this subject would have seemed to me damning. For this is an objection that arises within the causal view of anger. But outside of that view and *within* the agentive view, the story is otherwise. In anger, a person perceives herself and her circumstance in a particular manner—"under a certain description," as they say. This is not the accurate, agentive description that is available to others. She has intentions and motives, to be sure, but these pertain to the situation as she sees it. She might deliberate, she might forbear, but only in respect of *her* understanding of things. Hence she is not scheming about how she will assert or constitute herself as angry, make herself justified, provoke others to provoke her, or otherwise misrepresent herself. She is instead concerned about how to cope with provocation, whether to restrain herself, how much more she can take, why she has to be the object of such much calumny, etc. It does not follow from this that she is not doing what we can agentively perceive her to be doing: it does not follow that *her* understanding is correct. Otherwise, she would understand perfectly what she was doing and her self-deception would be impossible. (We must be careful to avoid question-begging.) So her trying to cope with and defend herself in a situation angrily perceived simply is doing what from a straightforward observer's point of view (which is a point of view she cannot have) can be seen as strategically and systematically making herself angry, victimized, justified, etc. In the end, all we learn from the objection is what we already know, that the agentive view of anger cannot be reconciled with the experience of anger.[10]

Assuming, then, that we have made legitimate our conception of anger as self-conscious action, we can say agentively that anger is defensive not in virtue of anything external, but in virtue of itself. The imputed anger-cause has powers to provoke anger if and only if it is perceived angrily. And now that we are able to say this much, we are in a position to formulate the fundamental question for this paper. What does this defensiveness consist in? How does her imputation of causality to an object explain the angry person's obsessive resistance to the demise of her anger, or in other words, her compulsivity in maintaining it?

DEFENSIVENESS, RESISTANCE AND OBSESSION

We seek reconciliation of anger's defensiveness with anger's resistance. To do so, we must account for the appearance the angry person gives of resisting admission of unconscious motives, but must do this without countenancing the existence of such motives. To explain why such a person is resistant and nurtures rather than flees his provocation, it is insufficient to say that making himself a victim is simultaneously making another his victimizer. This answer fails to tell us why he would not simply let the anger die and thereby divest the anger-object of its angering power. It fails, in other words, to account for resistance.

There have been accounts that abandon the phenomenon of resistance; mine would be such an account if I were to stop at the insight that anger is an assertion of an emotional kind

---

10   There is an interesting question that would take us in a different direction from the one I have chosen for this paper. When operating within the causal view of anger, the issue before us was: Anger is a judgment that proffers an explanation of itself; can this explanation be true? Within the agentive view an analogous issue is: Anger is 'self-constituting'; it is an act that takes of itself as not responsible for itself. Can this self constitution succeed? Can the angry individual ever coincide with what in her anger she takes herself to be? The answer, I believe, is that the more she tries, the more incongruent with herself her self image becomes. As long as human beings are angry, they are not, in spite of an existential cliché to the contrary, what they take themselves to be.

that asserts itself to be something that is, in fact, otherwise than what it is. On the strength of this insight I could have said that the angry person deceives himself about what he is doing by doing it in the sense that he eclipses for himself the truth about his act (and the situation relative to his act) in performing that act.[11] But in the absence of any other account of resistance, his only motivation for resisting would have to be the nature of what he deceived himself about, and of this (according to the view we are discussing) he has no inkling.

Another solution is only a little less unsatisfactory. It is this: Being angry means believing that one's provocation bears in upon one independently of one's own will or control. Given this perspective, "letting one's anger die" can only mean relinquishing one's defensive feelings and intentions and thereby leaving oneself defenceless against the provocation, which in this perspective, would retain its power to offend. As long as one's anger continues, one cannot see that abandonment would divest the anger-object of its angering power.

This answer tells why an angry individual would be unlikely simply to abandon his anger or let it die. But it does not tell us at all why he characteristically resists opportunities to let it die, e.g. when the object of his anger shows signs of withdrawing from the field of battle. We still need to know what there is about anger or its provocation that explains the phenomenon of resistance, and that does not, in explaining it, invoke unconscious processes.

We shall see that the answer is provided by the very property of anger that the causal view cannot account for. The threat A presents B cannot but be preposterous in B's eyes; (I spoke earlier of another reason for his outrage, namely, that he feels violated in his person.) Angry at him, A contends that he is maliciously or inconsiderately causing her anger and hence is not really angry at all, but feigning anger. But for his part, he knows

11 For an account of this type, see Robert C. Solomon, "Emotions and Choice," *Review of Metaphysics*, 1973.

directly that he *actually* has his anger feelings and is therefore not merely pretending. So her anger at him, which he reads as an accusation that she is feigning, has got to be preposterous in his eyes.[12] Surprisingly, it will turn out that the very absurdity (in his eyes) of the charges against him is the property that makes these charges indispensable to his anger. Their absurdity is an aspect of his sense of outrage. It is this that simultaneously presents him with what he sees as an external provocation *and* justifies the position he is taking (i.e. convinces him that his anger is genuine). Nor, as we shall see, is it necessary or even relevant that A is levelling these charges: anger is a self-troubling activity in which one cannot fail to feel both assailed and justified by such preposterous charges, irrespective of what the anger-object is actually doing.

I take it that the strength of the argument I shall offer resides partly in its explicit Wittgensteinian recognition that anger is essentially avowal, which is to say a kind of conduct, rather than an inner experience of which angry expressions are some kind of report. To think it an experience, as B does, is to assess one's expressions on the basis of their accuracy, i.e. their truth: hence, in his own eyes, B has got to be right in the argument because he *really is* angry. But as Harré has pointed out repeatedly, the correct assessment of social acts is not in terms of truth but rather of sincerity. B is unjustified not because he is giving false reports of his inner state, a charge he knows to be preposterous, but because in the avowing conduct that is his anger (which includes his continuous monitoring of that conduct) he is insincere, dissembling.

In order to make my case, I shall offer a series of observations, each of which provides only an aspect of the total account of these matters. At the conclusion of this section it

---

12 There is no doubt other reasons why his anger, with its implicit charges, is absurd. For example, as Harré has pointed out to me, it undercuts the conditions of personhood and respect of personhood on which the relationship is constituted, and also, obviously, the possibility of the altercation they are having with one another. But this sort of absurdity is not blatantly held before B's attention, like the (perceived) accusation that he is merely feigning.

should be clear why I say that the very preposterousness of the charge, in B's eyes, is what makes it essential to his self-justification.

Anger's Presupposition

Recall that B regards his anger-feeling not merely as not his responsibility, but rather as not the sort of thing which *could* be his responsibility. Given his view of it in having it, it is not the sort of thing he could produce in himself by taking thought, exerting his will, etc. Hence, in maintaining this view of his innocence and passivity in regard to his anger, he *presupposes* that he either (1) has the anger-feeling and is innocent and passive or (2) is not passive and does not have any anger-feeling at all, but is instead feigning his anger with an intent that can only be cynical and malicious. In other words, he presupposes that if he is not right about the cause of his anger-feeling—if he rather than A is responsible for it—then he hasn't got that feeling. But if he has got the feeling, then (in the absence of a mistake on his part, which, as we have seen, is a possibility he would in his anger reject) she is causing it. The agentive possibility, that he is responsible and yet has the feeling, is not a possibility as far as he is concerned, since the feeling is not, in his view, the sort of thing he could be responsible for.

A Falsified World

Agentively speaking, both alternatives in the disjunction he presupposes (sincere or feigning) are false. Thus it is that anger brings into being not simply the interpretation of itself that it asserts to be the case and that is false, but a complement of alternative interpretations of itself which are both false. It is this 'horizon' of possibilities taken together—it is the entire *outlook* in which the agent, B in this case, is either to be justified because innocent or condemned because malicious—that is the content of the angry person's self-deception. His self-deception is in this sense the falsification of the world, rather than simply the falsification of a situation within the world. That is, what is false is not just what he asserts about himself and his situation, but what he presupposes by that assertion.

Since as far as he can tell this outlook exhausts the possibilities, he cannot consider the agentive truth (which is that he is the author of his anger) without giving it a false interpretation. On his interpretation this truth can only mean that he is not really angry at all, but cynically pretending, whereas the agentive interpretation of this truth implies no such thing. His exhaustive horizon of false possibilities stands over against the truth about himself, which is not included in this horizon. The truth lies beyond the array of possibilities he can conceive. Correlative to this excluded truth about himself—B in this case—is the excluded truth about the anger-object, A, who for B must be either malicious or at least callous (if B is justified), or else caused to be angry by a malice of B's own (if B is not justified). In fact, A, the anger-object, is neither of these. The issue in B's mind is: Who is culpable here, A or I? Whereas the real issue is: Is the issue what B thinks it is? If he were not angry, would culpability be the issue? The answer is, No. That the issue in his mind is guilt and innocence is a function of his anger: a self-deception. The supposed cause for this effect does not exist apart from the effect itself. B will not be free from self-deception until this ceases to be the issue: until he is no longer angry: until he can perceive malice, if it is there, without perceiving offense.

Self-constitution as Denial

Now the self-condemning alternative to his anger judgment about himself and his anger-object is for B not merely an abstract or unsuspected possibility. That is, in constituting himself A's victim he does not merely constitute a spectrum of alternative possible interpretations of his apparent anger, only one of which is his concern. On the contrary, constituting himself a victim is constituting himself as *not* being a victimizer. One cannot maintain mere innocence, mere justifiability, mere sincerity, or, more obviously yet, mere freedom from responsibility. To undertake such self-assertiveness presumes that a question is being raised. A self-forgetful individual can be what he is, e.g. sincere or innocent, without regard to what he is not. But asserting or constituting oneself sincere or innocent by one's anger can only be in respect of some presumed (or presumed pending) charge. One can maintain one's innocence only by raising the issue of whether one is guilty (or acknowledging that issue if it has already been raised); one can maintain one's sincerity only by raising (or acknowledging) the issue of feigning; one's justification, the issue of culpability, etc. It is as if one asserted the favourable alternative by denying the unfavourable alternative - as if anger were a non-verbal way of saying: "I am *not* the kind of person who could be morally responsible for this."

The general point I am making is a central and poorly appreciated cornerstone of Sartre's conception of bad faith: self-constitution is actualizing one particular possibility over against others in a spectrum of possibilities all raised together by the act of self-constitution itself. The particular form of self-justification we call anger is a denial of being the sort of person who is insincere or malicious. Negation mediates the self-approval implicit in anger. One is not merely sincere, but sincere as opposed to feigning, etc. To be angry one must, in Sartre's words, become "a Not upon the face of the earth."

The Indignation in Anger

Let us move one step further. It might be thought that B's insistence upon his victimhood and his consequent innocence involves a denial of his culpability only in the sense of entailing it conceptually, so that all I've said could be true without B's actually being sensible of the condemnatory interpretation of his conduct that he denies. But in fact this interpretation is one he feels the urgent need to deny, as if he were in the dock. The substance, as it were, of his accusations of A and his indignation in response to her accusations of him is his effort to exonerate himself in respect of whatever it is he is blaming her for, and this cannot but take the form of an active denial of his culpabiltiy in this very respect. A is defaulting on the psychological contract he and she have together, not he; she, and not he, is the agency behind his wounded responses and her purportedly wounded ones. So B raises *in his own mind* the troublesome possibility he denies in the very act of denying it. His maintenance of his innocence and her guilt is equally a denial of his own guilt and of her innocence. His is a *self-troubling* act. This point crucial for establishing that what B is defensive about and resistant to admitting—what seems to motivate his over elaborate protestations of innocence—is not pre existent to or even independent of his denial of it, but an aspect of that denial.

So B is engaged in defending himself against the most intimidatingly personal kinds of charges completely apart from whether A, his anger-object, is actually levelling any of them against him, or even knows of his existence. In itself, anger is a kind of paranoia; just in virtue of being angry an individual conjures all the adversaries he must have in order, in his own eyes, to be angry justifiably, which is the only way one *can* be angry. His insecurity, then, his wrestling with self-doubt and guilt, his struggle to overcome a perpetual sense of unworthiness—all these are not less agitated, concerned, or energetic than his anger itself, because they *are* his anger. The sense of being violated as a person, in regard to one's rights, is equally nurturing of the violation: a kind of self-induced social disequilibrium. A judgment always implicit in one's anger, and as central as any other, is , "I am not wrong about myself." This judgment is implicit in such exclamations as: "Look, I mean what I say!" "I'm not just kidding." "Why do you think I've been sobbing for the past week?" "Don't think you're going to get away with this!"

It is in this way, then, that the agentive view accounts for his defensiveness. The angry person feels an urgency to defend himself against a possibility that (contrary to his belief) does not arise independently of his anger. There is a necessary connection between his denial of the possibility that he is a fraud and the urgency he feels to deny it. His self-deception does not consist in *directly* rendering the truth about his action inaccessible (by an internal act such as repression, for example), but in his creation of a possibility he feels a need to resist, which possibility, together with his asserted victimhood, excludes the truth.

Apart from this necessity, there are other reasons why B will tend to be defensive. For example, he will tend to construe any circumstantial evidence that is discrepant with his story as an attack upon his integrity. Obviously, if A is reciprocally angry at B, he will understand her anger—her self-defence against him—as an attempted condemnation of him; we have seen that this is because of the presupposition of his anger. But he will construe discrepant evidence in this way even if she *isn't* angry and therefore is not an accomplice to his anger. Since she *cannot* cause his anger-feelings in the way he supposes—they are constituted by him—she is necessarily innocent of his accusation against her. She is innocent not in virtue of anything she is or isn't doing, but in virtue of the nature of his anger itself. She is innocent in virtue of what *he* is doing. But this is an extraordinary sort of innocence he cannot possibly comprehend, precisely because he cannot (as long as he is angry) comprehend his anger as his activity. It is an innocence that consists in her being *neither guilty nor innocent* (in his sense of 'innocent'); that is, it consists in her being incapable of producing his anger because that anger is not the sort of thing external events can cause. But to him this extraordinary innocence—"incapable of producing it in virtue of the kind of thing it is"—can only be misunderstood by him as the more ordinary innocence "capable of producing it without actually having produced it." Thus any evidence that his accusation is not fully founded, any suggestion that A might be innocent in the first, extraordinary sense, will unavoidably be perceived by him to be evidence of his innocence in *his* sense-the ordinary sense—and *therefore* as an accusation of feigning, an attack upon his integrity, etc. All discrepancies or dissonance between his story and the circumstances threaten to condemn him, whether or not anyone means them to—and certainly whether or not they in fact do, for they do not!

We can learn something about the pressure to condemn himself that an angry person like Brent defends himself against by noting that sometimes, manoeuvring within the horizon of his self-deceived world, an individual will pre empt this pressure by denouncing or even berating himself. We take Brent as our example because, as the preceding bits of dialogue show, he is the one most prone to self-flagellation.

B.   It's too painful to be dragged through all this again.

A.   Here we go again. You pick a fight and then accuse me of hurting your feelings.

B.   Look, I know you think you could have married a more successful person.

A.   If you start on a pity party again, I'm going to walk right out of here.

B.   I shouldn't have picked the fight. I don't know what's the matter with me.

A.   I can't stand you being such a wimp.

B.   When I get mad at you I guess it's because I think you can do everything and I can't do anything.

A.   I'm going to take my shower, Brent . . . .

B.   I wasn't really mad. I don't know why I do it. I guess I just resent not getting ahead in my job as fast as you are.

This self-deprecating "turning inward" of the anger has its own self-righteous satisfactions. When he needs to, Brent can say: "At least I'm being honest with myself now." If he makes the ploy that he rather than Alison is morally inferior, his excuse for his moral shortfall is just as effective as any superiority ploy might be.

The constant possibility of this self-humiliation tells us something about the indignation of someone like Brent when he is not condemning himself. He is, he believes, suffering at A's hands—yet in spite of this, as we just saw in the discussion of innocence, he feels a claim is being constantly made against him on her behalf. He feels what he construes to be a 'moral' summons or demand to recognize and acknowledge this claim. He is experiencing a pressure, counter to his claims on behalf of himself, to abandon those claims in the name of honesty. From his perspective, this would require him to make no consideration for himself in virtue of his suffering (which he is sure is real), but to give every consideration to A, whose conduct is wounding and angering him. It is no wonder that "duty" for him is onerous. It calls upon him to relinquish his rights of protection and redress, to humiliate himself by conceding the claim presented on A's behalf that she is innocent. If made, this concession would be humiliating because, from his point of view, it would not be made in virtue of her conduct, i.e. because her present conduct entitles her to it (remember, he feels she is wounding him). It would have to be made *in spite* of her present conduct—in spite of the fact that she is wounding him. This means the concession would be made in virtue of something besides her conduct—for example, A's person, her rights or status, her inheritance, perhaps even her sovereignty, any of which implies his inferiority in regard to this something and his exclusion from full participation in the system of rights that constitutes him the person that he is. This pressure B feels to demean himself contributes both to what seems to him the irresistible provocation of these demands—"How can I not be upset when she humiliates me like this?"—and to the justifiability of refusing these demands. "They require too much. They are outrageous. Only a fool would grovel at her feet the way she wants me to." (A similar story can of course be told of A's indignation.) Anger is indignant; it contains the seeds, at least, of paranoia, and also of self-hate. (This is true even, or perhaps especially, of those who angrily wield great power.) A possible next step for either party in *any* exchange of angry accusations is always something of this sort: "Oh yes, I'm always the one who is in the wrong, aren't I? (Quivering chin.) I know I'm not the sort of person who's good enough for you. I just wish you wouldn't rub it in, that's all."

The Neutralization of All Conceivable Opposition

The absurdity of the felt attack brings us to the question: Why isn't the attack scoffed at or ignored? Why is self-condemnation the only perceived option? The answer is, it is the very preposterousness of the perceived claims against the angry individual that in his eyes establishes him as authentically angry, innocent of fraud, and justified. He raises the self-condemning possibilities in a preposterous form, and it is this that creates his conviction that he is right. He is obsessed with the evidence against him because it is his justification, and yet contemptuous of it because it is absurd; it justifies him precisely *because* it is absurd. (I.A. Richards said: "Contempt is a well known defensive reaction.") The only conceivable opposition to the self-justifying claims the angry person makes is thus neutralized. We might say: the angry person nurtures this evidence against him by denying it, and precisely in order to be able to deny it. What other evidence could one cite for one's own sincerity and innocence than that the alternatives are preposterous? No other evidence could conceivably count. *We see that, without taking thought, even unconsciously, but because that is the only way he can see the situation,* the angry person indignantly considers the possibility of his fraudulence—he perceives it as a demand that he condemn and demean himself—and in the same stroke discredits it, because in view of his suffering it is preposterous.

On this account, no unconscious psychological process is involved in resistance. All the features of anger I have described are simply aspects of angry conduct responsive to others in a pattern of altercation expressed in a rhetoric of accusation and excuse. What is resisted is not a truth harboured in a consciously inaccessible psychical region, but the obverse of the act of resistance itself—a possibility raised only by denying it. We have not explained anger causally; instead, we have understood it as an act carried out as a component of an interactive pattern, anticipating and construing the responses of others.

SELF-DECEPTION

Bad Faith

In my critique of the causal view of anger I said that characteristically a person who is angry concerns herself with whether the object of her anger actually did what he is being accused of. She is exercised to deny that she is mistaken about the accused. Yet her point of view allows that there is a possibility that she is mistaken, and that if she is, there is no cause for anger. Why then is she resistant to the possibility of liquidating her anger by entertaining the possibility of a mistake? How does the agency view account for this?

The answer seems to be that from the angry person's viewpoint it is unlikely that any evidence against her position could suggest a *mere* mistakenness in judgment. If B had been trying to say something different from what A thought he was saying—something quite innocent—and if he had presented his case to her, she would have perceived his protestations as asking her to discredit her feelings and to denounce herself (unless of course she had abandoned her anger, or was in the very moment abandoning it). We have already seen why. What to us may look like an honest suggestion that she has judged mistakenly is to her the suggestion that she is the kind of person who would treat him perversely. I am not saying she cannot admit to being mistaken, but only that she will be giving up her anger if she does; hence, if she isn't giving up her anger we can understand why she isn't openly considering the possibility of being mistaken, and (as is our common experience) pointing out her mistakes isn't likely to dissuade her.

> B.   I didn't mean to attack you when I brought up the shower. I wanted to help. When I came home, I was feeling romantic and kindly toward you. That's the truth, Alison.
>
> A.   Oh, so I'm the one who picked the fight!
>
> B.   (Controlled voice.) No, I didn't mean that. I only meant that I wasn't trying to make you feel bad.
>
> A.   So I made it up, huh? Why would I make up such a thing? Do you think I wanted to ruin the whole evening with another ugly fight?
>
> B.   No. I'm trying to say that what you thought I said to upset you, I didn't really say, so there's no need for us to be angry with each other.
>
> A.   That's it! Just gloss it over. You come home and start talking about how late I am, after I've done all the work, and I'm supposed to say, "Oh thank you, my Lord, for pointing out my shortcomings to me." You expect me to believe you? You think I'd be upset if you hadn't come home making insinuations?

There can be no admission of mere mistakenness unless the angry attitude and conduct have been or are being abandoned.[13]

There is an intuitive insight in Sartre's work on bad faith for which we can now provide a conceptual explanation. He said bad faith is a determination in advance to be persuaded by inadequate evidence, to be unfulfilled by the evidence, to take as the normal ground for conviction a condition of being not quite convinced. In Sartre's work, there is no adequate accounting for this 'determination'. But the agency view provides an account. The existence of one's own anger-feeling (together with the logical obstacles to consider whether one might be mistaken) is enough in the angry person's mind to establish the culpability of the anger-object. *Post hoc ergo propter hoc.* What objective evidence there may be, one way or the other, is inaccessible as such. Given one's experience of a feeling that can only seem the effect of offensive conduct, it is all but inconceivable that one could be wrong.

> B. Ask Fred if I wasn't singing your praises when we were driving home.
>
> A. So what if you were? It was probably to make him jealous or to try to makeup for the bad things you've said about me.

In a sense, the evidence against the anger object is the anger itself. The angry individual is convinced *a priori* that the case against her *must* be deficient, and she contents herself with almost any supporting evidence, even though partial, inconclusive, speculative, or even imagined, that is validated by that conviction.

---

13 It is precisely because our accusing emotions, such as contempt, hate, sadness, self-pity, and embarrassment, as well as anger, *are* avowals and not merely inwardly held experiences reported by expressions of emotion that our beliefs do not determine our feelings. Cognitive therapy to the contrary, the beliefs ingredient in these emotions change only with, and not prior to, the relevant changes of emotion. (It might be possible to test this claim empirically.)

Notice too that however ill-founded or trivially motivated or irrational one's anger may seem to others—however easy it may appear to correct it with a little information—it is in one's own view a response to an affront or a wrong. There is no anger the angry individual does not experience as a passion for justice.

The Appearance of Unconscious Processes

In the study of self-deception, the trick is to take the phenomenon of resistance seriously without invoking unconscious processes. This I have done in respect of certain self-deceptive emotions. The account I have given of these emotions does not appeal to unconscious processes, yet it shows why such processes appear to be taking place. From a point of view that construes anger-feelings on a 'passive reception' model, the resistance I have described—resistance to the demise of the provocation—cannot fail to be thought of as resistance to admitting an unconscious belief, motive, or intention. What gives rise to this appearance of the effects of an unconscious is a genuine resistance, but it is not a resistance to admission of such motives. It is instead something in the angry person's interaction with the object of her anger that she resists, namely, a moral claim against her, the ludicrousness of which is the core of her self-justification. The accompanying appearance of an unconscious motive for resisting this claim is an artefact of her anger (and of the sympathy of observers); it is not an internally held truth that her act eclipses. There is much indeed that the angry person does not know about herself or her situation, as we have seen, but this does not reside in an unconscious. It resides instead in an outlook publicly available to everyone besides her—an outlook that she does not and cannot enjoy because of being angry. Thus, the agentive view accounts for resistance—indeed, the sort of resistance whose motives cannot be acknowledged—without appealing to anything unconscious.

One way to state the problem with the classical conception of self-deception is this assumption, which as far as I know has not been called into question before: What the self-deceiver resists (e.g. the possibility of her own malice and fraudulence) is the very belief about which she deceives herself. On this assumption the *only* mode of self-deception available is concealment from herself—e.g. relegation of a belief-content to a "level" not available to consciousness. This is because the assumption entails that the belief about which she deceives herself is the same that she would openly believe were she not self-deceived. To suppose that beliefs are thus invariant through a range of psychological states, from straightforward attitudes to self-deceptions, is to assume that self-deception is a matter of the *status*, such as a 'below awareness' status, of a belief. On the agentive view, on the other hand, what she resists in her anger— the possibility of her own malice and fraudulence—is not what she is deceiving herself about. It is not what she would believe upon coming out of self-deception. It is an artefact of the anger itself, and it would not be a possibility—it would disappear without the anger. Thus, what she denies in self-deception, like what she affirms, is not possible to deny (or affirm) apart from the self-deception. On the agentive view, her self-deception is not a matter of concealing a belief, but a matter, we might say, of believing perversely, and this in turn is a matter of participating insincerely in that 'form of life' in terms of which she learned to maintain herself as a person.

So now we know that self-deception must be possible because we know that anger is possible (and also the other defensive/resistant emotions). But we've always known that self-deception is possible; what we've needed to know is, *how* is it possible? And now we are faced with the same question about anger. It is true that the classical contradiction in self-deception theory is gone, but this minimal answer is not enough. We want to ask, if the agentive account is sound, why would one ever adopt the 'rhetoric' of anger and similar delusory emotions? We can't appeal to provocation to answer this question, since anger is the author of its own provocation. Why would self-justification be anger's desperate concern if the issue of whether one is justified in the anger does not exist without the anger? The surprising answer to this question I have treated elsewhere.[14]

14 C. Terry Warner, "What We Are," BYU studies, vol. 26, no. 1, 1986, pp. 39-63

II

LOCATING AGENCY

In psychology as in physics, we postulate systems of unseen entities to explain phenomena that otherwise would seem to us insufficiently intelligible. Proponents of what might be called "the new scientific realism" in the philosophy of the natural sciences[1]—and Rom Harré is among the best of these—have important things to say about the phenomena that guide the construction of theory and the way they guide it. These phenomena, the new realists remind

1 See Rom Harré, *Varieties of Realism* (Oxford: Basil Blackwell, 1986); R. Bhaskar, *A Realist Theory of Science* (Hassocks, Sussex: Harvester, 1985); I. Hacking, *Representing and Intervening* (Cambridge: Cambridge University Press, 1983).

us, are created experimentally. They are created by means of
interventions, which are conducted by investigators deploying
experimental devices, into the basic material, the "ur-stuff," of
the world, to which Harré gives the non-committal nickname
"glub." It's how the apparatus is built that determines the phenomenal "shape" of the glub in the experimental situation,
within constraints dictated by the glub's intrinsic character. The
apparatus as it were "mobilizes" the glub in some particular way.
(What makes an experimenter great is the ability to make nature do things it otherwise would not do, in order to provide a
better basis for theoretical conjecture.) Thus the phenomena
that are most critical for theory construction exist only in conjunction with human intervention, and not in a pure state of
nature.[2] Harré quotes Niels Bohr—"No sharp distinction can
be made between the behaviour of objects themselves and their
interaction with the measuring instruments,"[3]—and adds: "We
cannot single out an aspect of the apparatus/glub meld and as-
sign it to some hypothetical object as [a] property of which the
reaction of the apparatus might be a measure."[4] This is one of
two insights from the new scientific realists I want to make use
of. The second one is: Though nothing is known of the glub
apart from experimental intervention, we do know something
about it in connection with such intervention. We know that
it possesses causal powers to produce particular experimental
effects when manipulated in particular ways. It might not be
going too far to say that, strictly speaking, it's not to account for
the phenomena, but to account for these powers, that scientists
speculate on the hidden structures and operations of the glub.

I want to use these two insights to elaborate upon what
Harré says in his paper about the powers of persons. To most
experimental psychologists, talk of such powers will sound like
Vitalistic hokum, indistinguishable from the embarrassingly
"unscientific" idea that a metaphysical will, mind, self, or soul

2 See Hacking, op. cit., for a cogent exposition of this view.
3 N. Bohr, *Atomic Physics and Human Knowledge* (New York: Wiley, 1958), p. 61
4 Harré, op. cit., p. 305.

is the producer of human behaviour. For such psychologists a Materialist metaphysics is essential if psychology is to emulate physics; that is, the hidden entities to which it ascribes causal powers must be capable, in the end, of complete physical realization. And whereas the internal processors of cognitive psychology presumably qualify by this criterion, Vitalistic powers do not. But Harré has in mind nothing so naive when he speaks of personal powers. His argument is that this way of emulating physics is misguided, and that a well-informed emulation will not ascribe the powers productive of action to such processors, but to persons. What he means by "persons" is grounded in his impressively informed philosophy of physics and must not be confused with the Vitalistic notion psychology rightly rejects. It's a more scientifically sophisticated kind of psychology he is advocating, not a more naive one.

HOW EXPERIMENT AND
SOCIAL ACTION ARE ANALOGOUS

The powers in question are not powers to produce every response human beings make, but only powers to produce the distinctively personal responses. By distinctively personal responses, I mean those responses that are informed in one way or another by speech. (Some may prefer to talk in terms of what speech expresses, which we often call rationality, and others of the rule-following or norm-adhering aspects of action.) These responses are "speech-informed" in the sense that whether or not they are speech-acts performed by utterance of words, they involve judgments, such as assessments and anticipations, of a complexity that only linguistically endowed creatures can produce. Examples include throwing a tantrum, which is an over-compensatory protest that someone else's conduct is both unfair and intractable; acting coy, which is a kind of manipulation by disingenuity; experiencing disappointment, anger, or resentment, which is an accusation that someone has defaulted upon his obligations; making a chair, which is based on an understanding of prevailing practical needs, tastes, and practices, including economic practices. I'm going to call all these "speech-informed actions."

Compare the production of experimental effects in the physics laboratory with the production of speech-informed actions. In the physics lab, there is the glub on one side and an experimenter, with his apparatus, on the other. The experimenter anticipates and is responsive to powers of the glub—powers to produce phenomenal displays of one kind or another, depending on the way the experimental situation is set up and the kind of apparatus employed. That is, the experimenter anticipates and is attentive to various possibilities of response, depending on what initiatives he takes. He designs his apparatus accordingly. The glub on the other hand doesn't anticipate, no matter how it happens to be structured. It doesn't respond to possibilities, but only actualities. It does its tricks only at the behest of actual causal interventions and never in consideration of possible causal interventions. It is indifferent to the experimenter's powers.

Now in the human situation, what stands in place of the glub, producing the phenomena we are interested in, is a being who is in every way like the experimenter, though usually unequipped with any devices comparable to the experimenter's apparatus. Unlike the glub, he isn't responding to actual causal interventions as he produces the phenomena I'm calling speech-informed actions. He's responding to possible interventions: he's anticipating all the time. He deals in the powers of his interveners.

One way to express this property of speech-informed responses is to say they are intervention-appropriating. Others' actions indeed play an interventionary role in the production of an individual's behaviour, as we shall see in a moment. But what that role is to be—how an intervention is to help shape his response—depends upon how he appropriates the intervention—that is to say, how he responds to others determines what their influence will be.

"But surely," someone will object, "if a person retaliates when pushed he's not responding to mere possibilities, to the powers of others, but to what's being called an actual causal intervention." This objection misses the point. If a person is pushed and he falls, he does indeed respond to an actual causal intervention, but his falling is not a speech-informed action. (I'm assuming of course that his falling isn't a deliberate display of falling on his part, to show that he was pushed.) But if on the other hand he retaliates, he will be regarding the pusher as able to do otherwise and therefore morally responsible for what he's done and deserving of punitive treatment; that is, the person pushed will be responding to the pusher in view of the pusher's alternative possibilities. He'll be responding to him as to a being possessed of powers.

In light of these remarks, some will wonder why we should say a person engaging in a speech-informed action is being intervened with at all. "Why can't we think of people as a lot of relatively autonomous aspiring interveners running around, each doing his own thing insofar as he engages in speech-informed actions and being done by only insofar as he is the victim of actual and direct causal intervention?" The answer to this question rests upon several considerations that will emerge in the course of my argument. I'll try to show that speech-informed action essentially involves others and can't be generated autonomously. By saying it essentially involves others, I'm saying not only that it is essentially intervention-appropriating, but also that there must be interventions by others to appropriate. Though the deeper reasons for this must wait, I'll say preliminarily that it is partly by being treated as one who can respond intelligibly and responsibly that an individual is able initially to acquire his repertoire of actions in the first place—that is, it is partly by being treated as one capable of entering into various ongoing social practices that one learns how to treat others as similarly capable.[5] Moreover, this mediation of one's conduct by the interventionary influence of others is not just developmen-

5 See J. Shotter, *Social Accountability and Self-hood* (Oxford: Basil Blackwell, 1984).

tal, it is on-going. For speech-informed actions are realizations of culturally prevailing forms of conduct, or variations of these forms; such forms regulate action in the mode of established social practices involving others. Hence to learn to perform an individual action is to enter, with others, into a practice by taking up a particular role *vis-a-vis* the roles of the others (and this is true even if one is seeking to revise or overthrow the practice, or to mislead others about one's intent). It is primarily in this way that the mediation of others' interventionary influence is an essential part of social action. It is only in the continuous interplay of people in shareable human activities that individual action is possible.

Here's another objection: "What if an individual is doing something ostensibly by himself—in an isolated cabin, say, in the mountains?" Of course this objection would be unanswerable if the intervention required were the sort of actual causal influence that activates the powers of the glub. But because being intervened with in the human realm is intervention-appropriating, there can be a kind of social action at a distance. A mountain man for thirty years alone still acts out parental conflicts, or strives to please or defy a father's expectations, or seeks to prove himself right or at least self-sufficient in his decision to live apart, or rejoices in his freedom, or is relieved to be away from hassle, or gets lonely, or is fearful or hopeful of the possibility of visitors, etc. There's no such thing as speech-informed action in a social vacuum. Because a person appropriates the interventions of others as part of what he does when he acts, we can follow the physics example and say this: The phenomenal display which we call his action exists only in conjunction with others' interventions—insofar as these interventions are appropriated by him. This, I take it, is one of the lessons we should have learned from the work of the great social psychologists Cooley and Mead.

SELF - MOBILIZATION

Now to say, as I have, that a person is intervened with only insofar as he "appropriates" the intervention is to break down entirely the distinction between the intervened-with and the intervener. In exactly the limited but legitimate sense in which he can be said to respond to intervention, his response is itself an intervention. He interveningly appropriates others' interventions. He's intervened with only insofar as he's an intervener. This is a stilted way to say that he and others are involved in common social practices in which each, in order to do what he does, absolutely relies on what the others do.

So when we say an individual, A, responds to the powers in another being, B (that is, when we say that A interveningly appropriates the appropriating interventions that can be ascribed to B), we are in effect saying that A treats B as a social being, a person, and not merely as a complex natural object. And part of what this means is that A treats B as having powers to treat A as a social being also, i.e., as one having such powers himself. In engaging in any action at all A sets himself to act in a manner that depends upon how B will react, and presumes that B will be making the same sort of assessment of him.

From this we can draw a significant inference: A acts as much in consideration of his own powers as he does in consideration of others'. He anticipates how they will respond to his response to them. Hence it's not enough to say that his act exists only in conjunction with their intervention. It's necessary to say also that it exists only in conjunction with his own intervention into his own ongoing condition. (He makes this intervention by appropriating the interventions of others into his condition). He indirectly or mediatedly appropriates his own intervention by this very intervention. Just as the experimenter mobilizes some sector of the glub by means of his experimental intervention, so the agent mobilizes a sector of the glub, namely himself, including the organism of which he's physically composed. But in his case, the mobilizing act is mediated by consideration of others.

He intervenes with himself by way of intervening with others, in that peculiarly social way that one person can intervene with another.

What we have here is a kind of "self-mobilization." It is what can rightfully be called the exercise of agency, the deployment of personal powers. It's a kind of self-intervention that could not be achieved by an individual acting upon himself directly, or reflexively, without the intermediation of others—that is, self-regulation cannot be an individualistic sort of undertaking, but is instead a kind of corollary of actions directed toward others. Only a being who is social in this sense can be self-directive in this sense. We are able to mobilize, direct, and regulate ourselves only because we are essentially with others—because our actions are anticipations of response to themselves.

There is nothing comparably self-directive in the purely physical world, simply because no purely physical beings are social in the sense I've defined—they don't respond to beings as having powers to respond to them as having powers. It's precisely for this reason that the powers to produce speech-informed action cannot reside in any asocial organization of the glub—for instance, in an unsocialized organism. Thus it's not because of what they are made of that the hidden generative processors or mechanisms of the psychoanalytic tradition, cognitive psychology, and Chomskiam linguistics can't possess the powers to produce speech-informed action. It's because they are conceived to operate individualistically.

AGENTS AND ORGANISMS

It's at least partly because of this individualism that there's been resistance to accepting the idea that persons are the beings that are psychologically real. Obviously, if an individualistically conceived person is not just an organism, then as I said before, it's got to be some non-material (and hence scientifically repugnant) Vitalistic entity, like a mind or spirit or will or self.

And thinking of the person this way raises the question of how he or she is related to the organism we associate with it. On the other hand, how are we to deal with this question if persons really are social rather than individualistic? To address this question I need first to comment further on what it means to be a social being.

Though phenomenal displays in the physics lab are the creations of experimental interventions—in a sense, these displays are artefacts—the processes of the glub presumably continue on whether we intervene with them or not (though what happens is not the same as when we do intervene). But there is no continuance of social processes in the absence of intervention. That is, in the social world, it's not just the phenomena that exist only in conjunction with intervention; it's also the beings that produce those phenomena. For these beings, persons, are essentially mutually interventionary; they are, one might say, artefacts of intervention. It's not simply that we know nothing of one another or of ourselves except insofar as we're intervened with and intervening; it's that we are nothing apart from such interventions. Persons are organisms that are being mobilized in a complex linguistic intermediation by which they invest one another with powers that organisms as such could not possibly possess.

None of this implies that persons are fictitious or epiphenomenal, any more than the phenomenal displays in experimental situations are fictitious or epiphenomenal—that is, the fact that they don't exist in a pure state of nature is no count against their reality. To exist only in conjunction with interventions of social beings is no second-class existence. It's instead the existence of a being that's not an object with defined spatial boundaries, but is instead an active appropriation of social influences. (Nor is it merely a nodal point in a social network; instead, it's an active contribution to the creation of such a network.

What then is the relation between persons so conceived and the organisms with which we associate them? Harré's answer to this question has two parts. The first concerns the relation of a causal power to its grounding state. The powers that produce the effects manifest in physics experiments belong to whatever system of beings the glub consists of; this Harré calls the grounding state of those powers. As a special case of this, the powers of an organism, which physiologists study experimentally, belong to the systems of entities of which the organism is composed. The powers involved are powers of that system; the system is the powers' grounding state. But in social intercourse the situation is different. There are personal powers, as we have seen, and there is a system of entities, the organism, that provides a physical grounding state for those powers. But this organism is not the being to which those powers belong. The being to which they belong, the agent or person, is a social being rather than a physical one. And that is to say, personal powers have a social grounding state as well as physical one.

What then is the relation between the social being and the organism? Consider this question in the spirit of Harré's paper.[6] When an action is appropriate to the social situation, making this appropriateness clear is, as Harré says, the way we give an accounting of it. Sometimes doing this requires recourse to the agent's social status or condition—for example, his legal authority in the situation, his disgruntlement, his diffidence, his lack of social skills, his trustworthiness or guile, etc. In such ways are entitlements, excuses, indictments, and other forms of moral assessment made. But when an action isn't appropriate, what may be required is reference to the agent's physical state— for example, his headache, his energy level, his nervousness, etc. Where particulars of the social grounding state are added it is still an action that is being accounted for; establishing appropriateness is still the aim. But where particulars of the physical grounding state are added, we are in effect qualifying the sense in which we are willing to call it an action; we are indicating some way or other in which the individual's agency is disengaged

6 See R. Harré, "Explanation in Psychology," in Daniel N. Robinson and Leendert P. Mos, eds., *Annals of Theoretical Psychology*, vol. 6 (New York: Plenum, 1990) pp.105-24

or aborted or compromised. Thus it is to the social entity, the person, that powers of action belong, and not to the physical entity. The person is both the social ground and the possessor of powers, whereas the organism as such is only a ground. In social action, the social grounding state is tied to personal powers in the same manner in which the physical grounding state is tied to natural powers, whereas the physical grounding state plays a role different from the one it plays in the production of phenomena in the experimental situation.

SOCIALLY LOCATED REGULATIVE SYSTEMS

There's a second part of the answer to the question about the relation of a person and his powers, on one hand, and, on the other, the organism we associate with him. He by his powers mobilizes himself—he mobilizes, that is to say, the organism of which he is physically composed by mobilizing the person of which he is socially composed. In this process he is guided by the forms of social action he's drawn from his cultural locale and deploys in his own idiosyncratic way. Via the deployment of his powers, the forms function as a complex regulative or control system that gives shape to his various public behavioural displays and to the physiological transactions that are the grounding states of this behaviour.[7] By this social process there are phenomena—actions—produced that never would or could be produced by any asocial organism no matter how complex, but always within constraints imposed by the intrinsic physical character of the organism. This regulative relation is no more problematic than the relation of the conception of the experiment, the apparatus, and the method of its deployment to that region of glub to which it is applied, because of which phenomena are produced that never occur outside of the experimental situation. Hence the social forms and the powers that realize

7 See R. Harré, D. Clarke, and N. DeCarlo, *Motives and Mechanisms: An Introduction to the Psychology of Action* (London: Methuen, 1985).

them are not mere conceptions or epiphenomena playing on the surface of a physiological reality which proceeds according to its own closed set of laws. They mobilize the organism and regulate it socially, and what happens physically as a result would not happen otherwise. That's why persons qualify as having causal powers: they have social and physical effects, and hence are real.

Let me re-describe the situation in a slightly different way, again in hopes of championing personal powers by the method of demystifying them. Remember as I do that the sort of things we know by means of the experimental practices of physics are not processes taking place independently of our inquiry, but rather nature's reactions to ourselves and our experimental prostheses. In a sense even our experimental interventions are manifestations of socially operative regulative or control systems; it is through these interventions that these systems shape the behaviour of the physical systems we are studying. The social situation is analogous, only here we intervene in systems that are reciprocally interventionary, so that our interventions are applications of regulative or control systems that mediatedly give shape to the mobilizations of our own physical systems.

THE INTERNALIZATION FALLACY

Now that I've set out a social conception of personal powers or agency, I'll indicate briefly what seems the crucial issue separating Harré's position from the "hidden processors" view he rejects. The central issue is where the act-forms or rules governing speech-informed action operate. In the spirit of Harré's work, I have suggested that they are socially located—that they exist primarily in the form of expectations that persons make of themselves and one another as they interact. According to the hidden processors view, these act-forms or rules operate "in" individual psyches, guiding hidden impersonal generative processes that are presumed to take place there. The two positions are rivals. A full treatment of the question of personal powers must include not only an exposition, such as I've been trying to give, of what they are, but also a refutation of the possibility of such hidden processes. In his paper Harré sketches the strategy of that refutation.[8] Here I'll offer only a few comments.

Here is one repeated kind of criticism of the internal processors view: it's futile to suppose, as this view must, that speech-informed actions can be thought of as assemblages of bits of language, information, and/or movement--and that the assembly process itself can be thought of as governed by certain rules. Such bits are aspects of speech-informed action that have been taken out of context. The criticism is that this de-contextualization can't in fact be carried out—that identifying the bits requires a surreptitious appeal to the meaning they have in context. What they are depends essentially on their roles in speech-informed action, and doesn't rest wholly on any features they can be observed to have independently of those roles. This futile supposition commits a form of what Roy Harris calls "the internalization fallacy."[9] Applying the rules to elements of speech and informed action requires that these elements possess features that (*per impossibile*) require an anterior application of the rules. So in the internalizers' program, characteristics of full-blown speech-informed action are "read back into" the resources required for producing it, and in practice this means importing the social grounding of conduct to a (supposed) hidden interior of the person. It means endowing an individualistic grounding state, the psyche, with all the mediated properties that are unique to the social grounding state. Harré presents a form of this criticism in his essay and Harris' discussion of it is excellent.

I want to go beyond saying the components of speech-informed action can't be decontextualized. I want to say they can't be de-socialized either. Such action is irreducibly corporate; only persons are empowered to accomplish it, and

8 See R. Harré, 1990, op.cit.
9 R. Harris, *The Language Myth* (London: Duckworth, 1981).

persons are beings whose productions are always mediated by the productive powers of other beings like themselves. Even if it were possible to produce sentences and "behaviours" out of de-contextualized bits by following certain production rules— and I don't believe it is—this would be a far cry from engaging in full-blown social practices by performing appropriate actions that are anticipatory of others' equally anticipatory responses. Transferring the production of action into a hidden interior, whether psychological or physiological, not only requires a surreptitious appeal to context and an impossible role for production rules, it also requires a question-begging replication on that level of the social arena of action. The de-socialization issue is broader than the de-contextualization issue. Much more needs to be said about this subject, though not on the present occasion.

Both forms of the internalization fallacy involve another fallacious manoeuvre that's part of a serious misconception of the role of rules in speech-informed conduct. A rule cannot be applied except to an already interpreted situation; hence it must be possible to acquire a repertoire of action-forms without learning and applying rules for doing so. (Action-forms that do involve the application of rules, such as mimicry or criticism or revision of existing expectations, would not be part of such a repertoire.) It's one thing to learn to speak one's native language, another to learn to speak a second language by applying certain explicit rules, usually including crude translation rules, and yet a third to speak that second language with facility, no longer needing to deploy any production rules. As Harré, following Wittgenstein (and I think guided by Baker and Hacker's important interpretive work)[10] correctly insists, a rule is formulated by observation of behaviour the production of which may not involve the deployment of that rule or any other; the formulation is then employed prescriptively and may (or may not) also be prescriptively expressed. The internalizers' program makes the mistake of supposing that just because a rule can be formulated

10 G. P. Baker and P.M.S. Hacker, *Wittgenstein Rules, Grammar and Necessity;* Vol. 2 of *An Analytical Commentary on the Philosophical Investigations* (Oxford: Basil Blackwell, 1985).

to capture a regularity of conduct, that rule must be operative in the production of that conduct—if not "consciously," then in the secret workings of the mental or physical system of which the individual is composed.

IMPLICATIONS FOR PSYCHOLOGY

In the ways I've tried to elaborate upon here and in a number of other ways, Harré is pressing for a reconsideration of psychology's emulation of physics—not as often happens for the purpose of discouraging it, but rather to fortify it by correcting its characteristic errors. If psychology is to become more like physics it must abjure its misguided positivism and root itself more sophisticatedly in appropriate adaptations of the actual practices of physics. Harré argues that we can't ignore the constitutive role of persons if we are to understand theoretical knowledge in the physical sciences. Persons engage with an independent reality to produce phenomena that manifest the powers of that reality and as persons are therefore crucial in the construction of that knowledge. And I've argued here that we can't ignore the constitutive role of persons if we are to understand social knowledge either. But in the social situation persons participate in the creation not only of phenomena but also, collaboratively, in the creation of the very beings whose powers are manifest in those phenomena. That is to say: They invest themselves with causal powers.

Because of its individualistic presuppositions, psychology has construed the idea of a person to be the idea of a non-material Vitalistic entity. And in the name of Materialism it has rejected this idea. Harré's social conception of a person is not a rival to Materialism, so the way is open for a respectable science of persons. This "personal powers without Vitalism" thesis is a neat solution to a long-standing debate. In sum: the subject-matter of psychology is not a system of natural objects, either seen or unseen. Because it has assumed otherwise, psychology has in some of its endeavours seemed a pseudo-science.

It can get itself on a scientific footing only by abandoning this assumption.

A solution like Harré's frees psychology from the sort of conceptual naivete that has kept its claim to scientific status perennially unresolved. Its practitioners have often engaged in a certain kind of rationalization wherein they narrowly and systematically re-characterize psychological phenomena in terms of what the generative processors they postulate are capable of producing. People like Harré are trying to endow it with a respectable philosophical rationale for considering the phenomena in all their social richness.

This is also a rationale for "humanizing" psychology practices—for treating experimental subjects not as impersonal mechanisms or processors, but as persons. For this solution shows us that to comprehend psychology as a science it is necessary to regard psychologists as belonging to the collaborative moral order of community practices—which means that the same requirements of consideration and appropriateness that govern conduct in that community apply also to them as they carry out their work. When the person of the psychologist is recognized as crucial to the work of psychology, as it must, it becomes clear that the onus is upon her to recognize the subject as also being a person.

III

SELF - DECEPTION AS VACUOUS EXPERIENCE

Self-deception is usually assumed to be that species of deception in which, instead of deceiving someone else, one deceives oneself. This assumption gives rise to the familiar conundrum: How can one and the same individual possess, as deceiver, the very beliefs that, as deceived, she lacks? (Sartre's memorable formulation: one "must know the truth very exactly in order to conceal it [from oneself] more carefully.") The failure of many philosophers and psychologists from Freud onward to answer this question, particularly since Sartre, cannot be blamed on any lack of ingenuity on their part. But none of them has realized that the question itself ought to have been rejected. For the assumption underlying it, that self-deception is a type of deception, is already a rudimentary, and untenable, theory of self-deception; I will call it the Standard Theory in this paper. This theory presumes a bifurcation of the self-deceiver's psyche into two functionally distinct parts; by some internal process or act, usually modelled on public intercourse between individuals, one of these parts deceives the other. This sort of split self is no more implicit in the idea of self-deception than in the idea of sitting oneself down. The split-self model, as well as the conundrum which gives rise to it, are products of the Standard Theory; neither is implicit in the idea of self-deception itself nor in any of the observations we all make of self-deceivers' conduct.

We need to start again, free of prejudice. We can do this by reverting to the conditions under which we are willing to say that an individual is deceiving herself. These conditions should cover those most problematic and central cases of self-deception which the Standard Theory was clearly devised to explain. Other cases, whether marginal or debatable, we can for the present purpose ignore.

I will specify a set of three conditions under which such cases occur.

1. Rationality. An individual makes a judgment that is decisively supported by her relevant beliefs.
2. In-supportability. This judgment is not supported, and very likely is falsified, by the relevant facts, where by 'relevant facts' we understand *what the individual would believe to be the case, relevant to this judgment, were she not deceiving herself.*[1] Typically the facts so defined are readily available to unselfdeceiving people around her.

---

1 I define the term 'fact' this way rather than in terms of truth because it is possible for a person to hold a belief self-deceivingly that happens to be true. We can imagine a Reverend Smyth (fl. 1940) deceiving himself into the belief that Gondwanaland did exist and was broken up and dispersed around the globe by continental drift, when every plausible scientific assumption and the preponderance of the available evidence indicated otherwise.

3. Resistance. The individual resists all suggestions that her judgment might not be true. Indeed she makes and maintains the judgment with an unwarranted insistence, an anticipatory resistance. Thus even when not actually being challenged, she holds the judgment as if she were.

Before showing how this set of conditions can be fulfilled without recourse to the Standard Theory, I want to examine briefly the way in which that theory comes into being through the alteration of this set of conditions, and mention one of its major flaws.

Conditions 1 and 2 entail that the individual's relevant beliefs—the ones that in her mind support her self-deceived judgment—are not the same as any of the relevant facts (what she would believe, relevant to her self-deceived judgment, if she were not deceiving herself). To the Standard Theory mentality this seems to preclude the possibility of Condition 3; that is, unless the self-deceiver actually believes, or at least strongly suspects, at least some of the relevant facts, she would have no motivation for resisting a suggestion that she might be mistaken. It appears that unless either or both of the first two conditions is amended, resistance is precluded, which is to say, self-deception cannot be distinguished from plain erroneous belief.

The Standard Theory typically amends Conditions 1 and 2 in this manner:

1. Rationality. An individual makes a judgment that is decisively supported by her relevant self-deceived beliefs.
2. In-supportability. This judgment is not supported, and very likely is falsified, by the relevant facts, by which we understand what the individual *unselfdeceivingly* believes to be the case, relevant to this judgment.

Presuming in this way that the self-deceived judgment is supported by one set of beliefs and falsified by another requires a bifurcation of the psyche, so that the two sets of beliefs will not summarily undermine each other, as they would if held (to use Sartre's phrase) "in the unity of a single consciousness."

Ironically, the strategy of modifying Conditions 1 and 2 precludes the very resistance it is intended to enable, for the first two conditions as modified entail that, insofar as the self-deceiver is deceived, she *cannot* be resistant. For they permit resistance on the self-deceiver's part only insofar as she unselfdeceivingly believes or suspects at least some of the relevant facts—and this is not at all the sort of resistance characteristic of self-deceivers. They resist they know not why; to put it in the confused language of the Standard Theory, they resist insofar as they are in a state of being deceived, not insofar as they are perpetrating the deception. If this were not so—if, as the Standard Theory has it, they were resistant in their capacity as deceivers—they would be nothing more than an ordinary liars or pretenders, and not self-deceivers at all. To avoid conflating self-deception with error, the Standard Theory inadvertently conflates it with ordinary deception.

Freud's bifurcated model of the psyche in all its versions suffers from this debility. In his clinical observations, it is *qua* conscious (that is, *qua* self-deceived) that the patient perceives and acts resistantly (is unaccountably defensive, fearful, or intrigued). Yet Freud locates the patient's motivation to resist elsewhere, in the Unconscious, and does this to ensure that insofar as she is conscious she remains self-deceived, i.e., innocent of her unconscious stratagems. Indeed, keeping her innocent in this respect is the function assigned to her unconscious acts of repression. But as I have already indicated this means precisely that, contrary to the observations that seem to license Freud's postulation of dynamically unconscious processes, she cannot *as a conscious agent* act resistantly.

Rejecting the Standard Theory's corruption of Conditions 1 and 2 leaves us with this alternative: The basis for the self-deceiver's resistance—the belief(s) upon which she acts when she resists—*cannot* be what I called a relevant fact (i.e., a belief which because of her self-deception she does not have but would have were she free of self-deception); it cannot be a belief or beliefs that, were she free of this self-deception, she would take to be true. On the contrary, the basis for her resistance must, by the logic of Conditions 1 and 2, be *false*. Accepting this implication of these two conditions fits better than the Standard Theory with what we know of self-deceivers, namely, that short of 'coming out' of their self-deception, when they consider the evidence relevant to their self-deceived conviction—and sometimes other people confront them with that evidence directly— they find confirmation of their conviction. This is only to say, tautologically, that one's having a particular conviction (together with other pertinent beliefs) self-deceivingly entails one's having that conviction (together with those other beliefs) self-deceivingly. The Standard Theory contains a contradiction because it denies a truism.

In attempting to make resistance plausible, then, standard theorists conceive of the self-deceiver as a being who appears irrational but is not, owing to her internal division into two functionally distinct beings in restricted communication with each other: internal mechanisms (her relation to which is left mysterious) prevent her from juxtaposing her conscious and unconscious beliefs and discovering their incompatibility. It is in this very odd sense that, on the standard view, the self-deceiver is rational. But as we have seen, being rational in this sense precludes the self-deceiver's resistance: her resistance requires that she be rational in the ordinary, straightforward sense (the sense in which one holds beliefs, if not always making sure they are entirely compatible, then at least not because, as the Standard Theory claims, some of them belie others, i.e., because they are logically incompatible.) As per conditions 1 and 2, the self-deceiver's consciousness must be unitary rather than bifurcated, for resistance to be possible.

This insight confronts us with the question I hope to answer in this paper: how, if self-deceivers must be rational in the straightforward, ordinary sense, can their resistance be made plausible? Once we have the answer to this question, it will not be difficult to see how an act that is decidedly possible, the act of self-deception, can consistently appear to be impossible—can appear simultaneously to be both ingenuous and disingenuous, a denial to oneself of a belief simultaneously affirmed, and can consequently give rise to the Standard Theory.

It is the very idea of the self-deceiver's straightforward rationality that suggests the direction in which we must look to reconcile it with the possibility of resistance. We must consider whether holding a certain kind of judgment commits the one who holds it to construe evidence against it in its favour, and if it does, under what conditions. I will suggest that by making such a judgment, an individual entraps herself in a system of false beliefs; so entrapped, she commits herself to misinterpret contrary evidence as untenable. And I will also suggest that the beliefs on the basis of which she resists challenges to her judgment are logically posterior, rather than anterior, to the act of making and/or maintaining this judgment. By stages I will set forth the features of this intellectual self-entrapment.

Surprisingly, we will find that it is in its power to account for the intractability of the self-deceiver that the self-entrapment view most outshines the Standard Theory. Standard theorists recognize this intractability clearly enough; they recognize that the self-deceiver cannot readily be dissuaded from her self-deceived convictions, even when explicitly confronted with the relevant facts. Yet their efforts to accommodate this essential and obvious feature of self-deception must be improvised. For how are they to foreclose upon the possibility of the self-deceiver's reflecting upon her act of self-deception, and discovering the truth about what she is up to? How can they keep her supposed self-deception from deteriorating, under introspection, into ordinary erroneous, readily correctable belief? The only way of doing this is to re-invoke the act of self-deception, as often as necessary; the self-deceiver is not only self-deceived in her original judgment, but also in any judgment she makes about that judgment, and any judgment she makes about these subsequent judgments, and so on. Thus to defend the possibility of an act that by their own admission appears to be impossible, standard theorists must invoke further iterations of that very sort of act. If they do not find this consequence unacceptable in itself they ought to remember that, given their bifurcation of the psyche, it only renders its 'conscious' sector more completely incommunicado, more irretrievably ignorant of the mental processes that guide the individual's behaviour, more innocent of any complicity in its own deception, more relegated to the position of one who is straightforwardly deceived, and therefore less plausibly thought of as being in a position to react resistantly.

A variant of this manoeuvre is to conceive of self-deception as the individual's refusal to form judgments, particularly about certain of her own mental activities and emotions. Here self-deception is thought of as motivated ignorance.[2] This version fails even more blatantly than the last to account for self-deceivers' intractability, for it eliminates at the outset all the most interesting cases, e.g., the case in which the self-deceiver is challenged with explicit formulations of the evidence against her position and earnestly denies them, and the case in which she crusades, again in earnest, against transgressions she herself is guilty of, talking about them herself in explicit terms and pre-

---

2 In his pioneering work Herbert Fingarette claims that we deceive ourselves by refusing to spell out to ourselves what we are doing when we engage in certain actions. We refuse to avow them. By this approach he seeks to avoid the Standard Theory's pitfalls; instead of taking up a psychical action to repress a belief, the self-deceiver refuses to formulate it (and of course refuses to formulate this refusal, etc.) Because this means that the moment of self-deception is separate from the act or condition that the self-deception keeps 'hidden,' Fingarette's theory is but a variant of the Standard Theory as I have formulated it. For it requires 'on some level' a recognition, if only rudimentary, of material not to be formulated.

senting herself as innocent of them.

These introductory comments about the Standard Theory reinforce our decision to begin, as we have, by assuming
the straightforward rationality of the self-deceiver. They make a
strong case for recasting the venerable but misconceived 'problem of self-deception' from: 'How is it possible to be both deceiver and deceived -to possess as deceiver the very belief that,
as deceived, one lacks?' to: 'How it is possible for one to hold
insupportable beliefs both rationally and resistantly? That is,
how can one, in maintaining such beliefs, appear to be motivated
by knowledge or suspicions that one's position is insupportable
while neither knowing nor suspecting any such thing?'

SELF-JUSTIFYING CONDUCT

By what sort of act of judgment might one deceive
oneself? What sort meets the three conditions I have formulated? As it turns out, a commonplace one. To call to mind those
of its properties that are relevant to our inquiry I will call it a
'self-justifying action' (the term 'warrant-claiming action' might
have done as well) and the judgments it makes, 'claims.' Here are
four of these properties:

> 1. It is an act by which its agent claims justification for
> it, or for herself insofar as she is engaging in it. It is, as
> it were, a self-excusing or self-justifying action.
> 2.   Strictly speaking, this claim is made non-ver-
> bally Whether or not words are thought or spo-
> ken in the process of making the claim (and none
> may be) the claim is made, as they   say, paralinguis-
> tically, by the manner in which the individual acts.
> 3. The claim always has an accusatory aspect, comple-
> mentary to its self-excusing aspect: the agent justifies
> herself by laying responsibility on someone else, or on

the circumstances, for the fact that she is engaging in this act.

4. The act of judgment, the action of making the claim, is an emotion.

Ordinarily we suppose that when one justifies oneself, one claims justification for conduct, past, present, or future, that is independent of the claim. But a self-justifying action of the kind I am interested in here makes a claim of justification for itself, or by means of it the agent makes such a claim for herself insofar as she is engaged in this action. The justification claim is thus self-referring; the action for which justification is claimed and the action of making that claim are one and the same action. And this is possible because the claim is made *by the manner or way* in which the self-justifier acts.

Each of the parties in the following domestic example is engaging in just the sort of self-justifying conduct I am describing. She compiles a list of weekend family activities. He mentally reserves Saturday for golf with his friends. During the week she drops hints, pressing him with an accusation in her voice that unmistakably expresses her slightly bitter conviction that he is likely to disappoint her yet again. He for his part rankles at this pressure and droops around the house, increasingly as the week progresses; anyone present can see that he believes himself a man oppressed. If he ends up going golfing on Saturday morning he storms out the door when her suggestions (his word is 'nagging') begin (as they are almost sure to do when she perceives his reluctance); "I refuse to take this abuse!" he mutters. And if he ends up spending the time with her he is hard-eyed, and his jaw is set on edge. To him, she is inconsiderate of his need to refresh himself with his friends. To her, he is inconsiderate of her need to have refreshment of her own after working all week just as hard as he has.

The actions of these people are carried out in the

self-presenting manner that Erving Goffman has called 'impression management.' By acting in this manner, they claim a warrant or justification for themselves. For example, the man in the story insists by his gait, his carriage, his flamboyantly hopeless gestures, his grim expression, his oppressed tone of voice, etc., that he is coping as best he can with insensitive treatment. He makes it clear that he is doing all that can reasonably be expected from a person so abused—indeed, that he is making sacrifices. His manner is *self-interested*; by it, he posts a claim on behalf of himself, about the moral quality of his conduct; he claims to be justified and possibly even commendable in what he is doing. And similar things can be said about the woman.

You will have noted the accusation implicit in their self-justifying claims. The man does not simply walk out and around the block or get in the car with the woman to go to town; he does these things pouting and slumping, showing in doing them how he suffers from her callous disregard of his hopes. He makes it clear that the reason he is justified in what he is doing in response to her is that she is not justified in what she is doing in response to him. He can disregard her requests, or respond begrudgingly, because (so he claims) these requests are insensitive and unfair. Without her culpability his resentment would be patently unjustified.

The woman for her part does not contend merely that she is justified in pressuring him; she contends that her pressures are justified because without them he will not do anything at all. It is precisely his treatment of her that in her mind justifies her in her treatment of him. Without his culpability her conduct would be starkly malicious. (Imagine her chagrin if in the middle of making one of her insinuations, flowers were delivered to the door, with an invitation from him for dining and dancing.) Thus her claim that it is within her rights to coerce him is simultaneously a claim that it is not within his rights to spend his free time doing whatever he pleases (and the same sort of thing is true of him). *Claiming justification for engaging in a self-justifying action entails accusing someone else of acting unjustifiably* (and a major part of what needs justification is this very accusation).

Besides being the making and maintenance of an accusing and self-excusing warrant-claim, the self-justifying action is equally the adoption of an accusing and self-excusing emotion. (Whether the converse is true—whether the adoption of such an emotion is the making of such a judgment -is an independent issue.) Examples of accusing and self-excusing emotion include of resentment, bitterness, anger, disappointment, jealousy, and humiliation. Such emotions are the means our culture has provided us of claiming that we are being wronged—that someone is violating our right to be treated as befits the kind of person we think we are. They are the means by which we assess a situation as unfairly unfavourable to ourselves and take offense. I am suggesting that it is only by means of the adoption of such an accusing, self-excusing emotion that one can take offense (that is, claim that one is being offended). (If the agent did not feel victimized in the very act of making the claim, it would be a mere rehearsal of words unconvincing even to herself.) Though a case might be made for the passivity of certain emotions, the emotions in which self-justifying actions consist are not among them. These emotions are claims actively made and expressed self-presentationally—not in their feeling aspect, of course, but in their adoption and maintenance. The self-presentation, the self-justification, the accusing, self-excusing emotion, and the claim-making are aspects of a single piece of conduct.

Some may balk at the idea that emotions such as I am discussing are acts of judgment. They may appeal to common sense: these emotions are not experienced as actions, but as arational or irrational and passive responses to provocations originating independently of the respondent's will. This, I suggest, is a self-deceived experience, to be explained by the account of self-deception I am about to offer.

THE NATURALISTIC PRESUPPOSITION OF
SELF-JUSTIFYING EMOTIONS

Though adopting and maintaining a self-justifying emotion is an action, the *experience* of this emotion is the experience of being acted upon, of suffering an affliction, not the experience of acting. Thus, such an action is systematically misunderstood by its agent; performing it is inherently self-deceptive. For the man in our story to become and/or stay angry with the woman is for him to believe that she, or what she is doing, is making him angry. Hence, though the action is his, and his responsibility, he experiences it as a passion—as the effect of *her* action and therefore produced independent of his will and not his responsibility at all. I will call this idea—*the self-justifier's idea that the emotion being experienced is an effect of external events, a passion rather than an action*— 'the naturalistic presupposition' of the self-justifying action. It is a presupposition both of and *about* this action.

My solution to the problem of self-deception as I recast it at the end of the introduction turns upon several implications of the fact that the self-justifier holds the naturalistic presupposition, two of which I will mention now.

First (given the naturalistic presupposition of her emotion), *the self-justifier cannot acknowledge any responsibility for her accusing emotion without giving the emotion up altogether.* Since it is a claim that responsibility for it lies elsewhere, if she were to acknowledge the responsibility to be hers she would by that very act give up her claim that it is not, which is to say, she would abandon the emotion.

Second, it follows that *any prospect of acknowledging that responsibility—of conceding that her claim is not true— would in her mind be the prospect of conceding that she is not in fact experiencing the emotion at all.* Given the naturalistic presupposition, either she is right in her assessment of the situation and is not responsible for that emotion, or else (in spite of her claims) she is not experiencing it at all. There are no other options.

I call the self-justifier's belief in the passivity of her emotion a presupposition of her action or judgment rather than an assumption because, from her point of view, it remains true whether or not her judgment, her justification-claim, is true. If the claim is true then she is not responsible for the emotion; the accused is responsible. But if the claim is not true then, as far as she is concerned, it does not follow that she is responsible and the accused free of responsibility. It follows, instead, that she is not and indeed cannot be responsible for it because, as we have just discovered, she cannot in that case be experiencing it at all. So either way, whether or not her claim is true, she cannot consider herself responsible for the emotion. She may concede responsibility for some of what she is doing, but this will not include maintaining the emotion.

THE INCONTROVERTIBILITY OF THE SELF-JUSTIFIER'S EXPERIENCE

We are now in a position to see why the self-justifier cannot fail to find in her experiences confirmation of her self-justifying claim, and these experience include her reflection upon her own emotion and state of mind, her public conduct, and the conduct of others. The reason she cannot fail to find this confirmation is that, given her naturalistic presupposition, she cannot discriminate between two distinct states of affairs involving the emotion and the claim it makes: The first of these states consists in the emotion's being experienced by her. The second consists in the claim's being true. In other words—and this is a third implication of her holding the naturalistic presupposition—*she cannot distinguish between truly having the emotion and having a true emotion, i.e. an emotion that makes a true claim.* Perhaps no feature of her self-justifying conduct has stronger implications for her self-deception than this, for because of it, the mere fact that she has the emotion with which she accuses another will in her mind suffice to confirm this accusation. In other words, her naturalistic presupposition so structures the self-justifier's experience that when she considers her emotional state or behaviour, or the behaviour of whomever she accuses, in order to determine whether or not her self-justifying judgment is correct, she will unfailingly find decisive support for that judgment. Far from ignoring or refusing to take note of matters relevant to it, she is preoccupied, and possibly even obsessed, with such matters.

Moreover, the logical limitation upon her experience imposed by the naturalistic presupposition leads her to construe her own behaviour as supporting her self-deceived conviction. For insofar as she entertains the possibility that her justification-claim might be false, she also must prepare herself to admit that her suffering behaviour is a sham. If that claim were false, she could not be experiencing the emotions she blames on others and therefore all her carrying-on about being right and others being wrong could only be so much dissemblance and malingering.

Consider again, as an example, the male in our case study. From his viewpoint, if he were to concede that he is not actually experiencing the emotion he claims to be experiencing, how could he then account for his pathetic gestures—his collapsing shoulders, his defeated silences, his eye-rolling grimaces and heavy sighs? They could not be expressions of how he really feels; they could not be what he presents them to be. They could only be so much empty show. The one possible interpretation of his conduct that his naturalistic presupposition allows, if he is not really experiencing the emotion, is that he is cynically posturing in order to have his own way at his companion's expense. This is the only possible interpretation because, as I have already pointed out, he cannot distinguish between experiencing

the emotion and being right in his claim that she is causing it—
if she is not causing it, he must not be experiencing it. So in
his mind, the alternative to his unqualified self-exoneration is an
equally unqualified self-condemnation. And this condemnation
he 'knows' (i.e. thinks he knows) to be preposterous, because he
knows he is really experiencing his emotion.

For this very reason he also 'knows' that his companion
is culpable. He 'knows' this in virtue of the 'evidence' in his pos-
session, namely, his offended feelings. Because he is not merely
pretending to have these feelings but actually has them, he does
not doubt that she causing them; he 'knows' she is intimidating,
angering, disgusting, embarrassing, humiliating, or otherwise
upsetting him. As far as he is concerned, his offended feelings
prove her offensiveness. Therefore, he is convinced, *she* cannot
possibly be sincere in her defence of herself, no matter how
vehemently she may claim to be; she has got to be the manipulative and cynically malicious one. *Post hoc ergo propter hoc.* The
manner of the self-justifier seems to pose this unarticulated and
fallacious rhetorical question: "Would I be trembling (flushing,
stressed, weeping, etc.) like this if you weren't offending me?"

The extent to which the naturalistic presupposition im-
poses limitations upon the self-deceiver's experience of herself
and of others is crucial in understanding self-deception. If *per
impossibile* these limitations applied only to her self-understanding, she would retain the ability to collect, by means of perceptions of her surroundings untainted by her concern to justify
herself, evidence against her conviction. But she does not retain
this ability; her naturalistic presupposition structures her experience of her circumstances, including her own and others' behaviour, as much as it structures her introspective experience of
herself.

Another implication of the self-justifier's holding her
naturalistic presupposition: *Since it is by her action—the action of
making the judgment—that the self-justifier adopts and maintains her*

accusing feelings, the person she accuses cannot be causing those feelings.
He might in some way provide an occasion for her to make the
judgment, but he cannot be a cause of the emotions she experiences in making it. On this count alone he is innocent of her
accusation. That is to say, his sort of innocence is contingent
not upon anything he is doing or not doing, but upon what *she*
is doing. Thus he is not innocent in the ordinary sense of the
word—not innocent as opposed to guilty. In the ordinary sense
he is neither innocent nor guilty. His innocence is, instead, of
a categorical sort. But this extraordinary sort of innocence can
only be misunderstood by the self-justifier to be the ordinary
sort, which is to say, to consist in his not doing what she accuses,
and perceives, him to be doing. To perceive him innocent in the
categorical sense, that is, innocent in virtue of what she herself
is doing, would for her no longer to be doing it—whereas she
is doing it. Therefore any evidence or consideration concerning his conduct, however tentative, suggesting that he might not
altogether be causing her emotion and that she is at least partly
responsible for it, must be understood by her as suggesting that
he is not doing the offensive things she sees him to be doing,
and that she is therefore not suffering at his hands. And this, as
I have suggested, she cannot fail to find preposterous. In her
mind, he must be mistreating her, must be guilty in the ordinary
sense, precisely because she is suffering and therefore 'knows'
she is not guilty in the ordinary sense. So any such discrep-
ancy or dissonance between her story and her perceptions of
the accused will *a priori* be taken by her not as undermining her
position but as confirming it. (Here we can begin to see how a
person can hold a belief defensively, as if resisting a challenge,
and do so in a straightforwardly rational way, that is, without
being motivated by any ulterior knowledge or suspicion of its
in-supportability.)

Necessarily, then (unless she abandons her self-justifying emotion, which she does not believe lies within her pow-

er), the self-justifier cannot openly consider any challenge to the adequacy of what she considers her supporting evidence. She cannot consider the evidence except as favourable to her case, because that case has carried the day in advance. This is why self-deceivers seem persuaded *a priori* that any case that can be brought against their position is *bound* to be deficient. It is also why they seem to content themselves with virtually any supporting evidence, however partial, inconclusive, speculative, imagined, or even irrelevant it may appear to observers. In the context of his own system Sartre uses the term 'non-persuasive evidence,' and here we are discovering that, though unpersuasive to others, it is decisive, nay, incontestable, to the self-deceiver.

THE PERCEIVED VIVACITY AND OBJECTIVITY OF THE EVIDENCE

In fact this evidence is vacuous, being a construal of the circumstances that is produced in conjunction with the very act of judgment it is believed to support. But to the self-deceiver it is no more vacuous than it is unpersuasive. Nor is her experience of it weaker or more tentative than other cognitive experiences. As experience, it is, to use Hume's terminology, forceful and vivacious. She perceives the evidence supporting her conviction to obtain 'out there,' in her circumstances, independent of her will.

For one thing, her self-justifying judgment about herself is (mediated by) a judgment about others—about them in relation to her and herself in relation to them. For example, experiencing humiliation is not simply having a feeling; it is believing one is being humiliated by some other person; it is believing that the conduct of that person is, in and of itself, degrading. The same sort of thing is true of feeling angry, offended, bored, disappointed, embittered, envious, jealous, disgusted, intimidated, etc. The self-justifier's judgment "magically transforms" the world (the phrase is Sartre's) into an unfair and threatening place where, through no doing of her own, she is suffering mistreatment. She believes she is perceiving in the surrounding world incontestable support for her claims.

What I have been saying about the mutual entailment of the self-justifier's claim for herself and her accusing regard of another does not imply she is merely imagining that the accused is humiliating her (though she might be). But it does imply that he cannot humiliate her unilaterally. Humiliating an individual requires 'uptake'; for one person to degrade another, the one being degraded must believe that the conduct of the other is degrading her. Humiliation is something (at least) two people do together—a corporate action, if you will. Therefore the degrading quality that the self-justifier perceives in the offender's conduct is precisely as internal to her self-deception as her own offended feelings. And again, all this is equally true of angering, embittering, disgusting, or otherwise offensive conduct. *The evidence appears to the self-justifier as substantial and vivacious even though, at one and the same time, it is vacuous, being a function of her holding the very conviction she believes it to support.*

There are other reasons why I say the self-justifier actually perceives the evidence supporting her conviction to obtain 'out there' in her surroundings. As I indicated earlier she can consider herself justified only insofar as she considers the conduct of the person she accuses unjustified; she can believe herself morally right only if she believes him to be morally wrong. Hence, given that in her mind she is his victim, she *cannot* simultaneously entertain the thought that he might be justified in his conduct. For if he were justified he could not be mistreating her, her accusation of him would be ill-founded and perverse, and she herself would be the one morally in the wrong rather than innocent of fault; she would have to admit to cynically playing the victim in an effort to make him feel bad and exonerate herself. And, as we have already learned, she 'knows' that she is actually suffering and not merely posturing. So when she looks at him or thinks about him, she does not contemplate a man who might or might not be guilty of her accusation. She contemplates one who, as far as she can see, is guilty. She perceives what he is doing as unfair, irritating, disgusting, infuriating, humiliating, etc.[3]

RESISTANCE

We have seen that, in the self-justifier's mind, being responsible for her accusing emotions implies that she is dissembling and cynically and maliciously using the person she is accusing. For this reason, insofar as she thinks about the matter, she comes to believe that she can accept this responsibility only by 'admitting' that she is thoroughly worthy of condemnation, and that by this 'acceptance of responsibility' she would be confessing to something she is not doing. But this patent falsity, in her mind, of the idea that she might be responsible for her accusing emotion—the idea that the accusation she makes by means of this emotion might be false—is *not* her reason for resisting the idea and clinging to her accusation. The falsity of an idea cannot explain resistance to it. On the contrary, anyone who seriously believed it false would not take it seriously enough to resist it. Were it said that you personally sabotaged Russia's chances for economic recovery you would very likely laugh, not vehemently resist. To the self-deceiver, the idea that she might be responsible for what she is experiencing is as least as preposterous.

Why then does she resist this idea? The answer is, *in the context of what she believes herself to be experiencing, this idea, that she might be responsible for her suffering contains an implication that is not falsified, even in her own mind, by the fact that she is suffering.* Her justification-claim is a claim that she has a right to be doing as she is

<hr>

3 This incidentally is why self-justifiers often seem to love their suffering and to experience a little thrill of triumph when they catch the accused mistreating them: it is further proof of their self-justifying claim. All these considerations indicate why the self-justifier experiences herself as a person virtually inundated by evidence in support of her position.

doing, and, correlatively, that the person she accuses has no right to be doing as he is doing. Her preoccupation, then, is with her rights in the situation and with the kind of person she would have to be in order to possess those rights (which means, with her social status as a person) and, correlatively, with the rights he does and does not possess and the kind of person he must be. So, given her suffering, she can only construe the idea that she is responsible for her emotion to challenge her justification-claim directly: *"You don't have the right to do as you are doing. You are claiming rights you do not have and transgressing the rights of another. You pretend to be a justified, legitimate sort of person when you're not. So in spite of your suffering—irrespective of the abuse you believe the other person to be dealing out to you—accept the blame!"*

Keep in mind that this cannot mean, for her, that she is blameworthy in virtue of either her conduct or his—that interpretation she cannot but consider preposterous, as we have seen. It can only mean she is blameworthy in virtue of something else entirely, apart from what she and he are doing. It can only mean she is blameworthy because of not having the rights she claims to have, because of not being the kind of person she claims to be. So the idea that she is responsible for her emotion implies, in her mind, her morally inferior status as a person, relative to whomever she is accusing, as well as his morally superior status as a person, relative to her. This idea says: *"Accept your unworthiness as a person! Exonerate him in spite of his mistreatment of you—just because he is superior to you as a person!"* (What else can she think?) In this way the suggestion that she might be responsible for her emotion seems to her to cut past her 'evidence' against it and condemn her on a plane more basic than any consideration of evidence. It cuts against her personal identity and calls upon her abjectly to debase herself before the very person she believes to be mistreating her. No wonder she does not appear to act reasonably. As far as she is concerned all her reasons have been put out of circuit by an irrational attack on her identity, status, and worth as a person, an attack that strikes a blow, not countenanced by the rules of evidence and argument, that she finds offensive in the deepest possible way. So though she 'knows' she cannot be responsible for what she is experiencing, this 'knowledge' is irrelevant to the attack she feels herself to be undergoing. *Thus does the suggestion that she might be responsible make her feel it necessary to defend herself even while failing to controvert her justification-claim.* (This is one reason why self-deceivers seem so often to take offense where none is intended, to make mountains out of molehills, and to refuse to ignore even minor inconveniences.)

INTERNAL RELATIONS

We have gone part way toward answering the question, Why would the self-justifier resist the idea that she is responsible for the accusing emotion that accompanies her justification-claim? But the answer is incomplete, for it is far from obvious that a self-justifier would take offense at the sort of personal attack I have just described. Some people, indeed, would not take the attack seriously; instead they might, either with disdain or compassion, think the attacker merely pathetic. This fact, that some would not take it seriously, might tempt us to suppose that we are faced with an empirical issue and to pass it to psychologists, expecting them to inquire under what conditions people are likely to take offense at a personal affront, and what personality types are most like to do it. But in my account of self-deception I am not speaking of everyone. I am speaking only of self-justifiers—those who are engaged in making what I have called self-justifying judgments. That they feel their social identity challenged is not a contingent matter. It is internally linked to—it is an aspect of—their self-justifying action. Their preoccupation with their justifiability and their feeling of being personally attacked come into being together. One cannot engage in a self-justifying action such as I earlier defined it without believing one's justifiability is being challenged and taking the challenge seriously. A self-justifying action *just is* a defence against such a challenge, whether or not anyone is actually making the challenge.

Therefore the self-condemning alternative to her claim is for the self-justifier not merely an abstract or indifferent possibility. In claiming herself another's victim she does not merely select one interpretation of the action from a spectrum of alternatives. On the contrary, she chooses one *by* denying another. To present herself a victim she insists, not necessarily with words, that she is *not* a victimizer. An individual unconcerned with justifying herself can simply be the sort of person she is, e.g. innocent, justifiable, sincere, or free of responsibility, without any regard to the possibility that she might not possess this quality of character. But one who presents, asserts, or stylizes herself as innocent acknowledges that her innocence is in question—she may even raise that question herself by her self-presentation—and similarly for the person who maintains her sincerity or her justifiability, etc. The favourable alternative is maintained by the denial of the unfavourable one, as if the claim, "I am innocent!" were an oblique and socially smoother way of asserting: "I am not the kind of person who could be morally responsible for this!" The general point I am making is a central yet unappreciated cornerstone of Sartre's conception of bad faith: what I have been calling self-justification—what he calls self-constitution—consists in actualizing one possibility over against others in a spectrum of possibilities all raised together by the self-constituting act itself. Negation mediates the self-approval implicit in the self-justifying action. One is not merely sincere, but sincere-as-opposed-to-feigning, etc. To justify oneself thus one must, in Sartre's words, "become a Not on the face of the earth."

(The fact that defence against condemnation is her perpetual issue might seem to suggest by turning her accusation inward and condemning herself, she can take herself out of the squirrel-cage of her self-deception. It is true that, because of her preoccupation with the possibility of her condemnability, she always has access to this option. But if she takes it, she will only vary her mode of justifying herself—as Nietzsche wrote, "To despise oneself is to love the despiser in oneself." She will divest herself of responsibility at least as neatly she previously did by blaming someone else. Her self-condemnation will include an implied accusation of others—e.g. for not coming to her defence; by it she will hold them hostage to her dejection or despondency, being so miserable that they would be crass indeed if they dared to be happy in her presence.)

In connection with being internally related to her anxiety over her moral acceptability, the self-deceiver's self-justifying act is internally related to her perception of whomever she is accusing. It involves her in seeing the accused as reciprocally accusing her. Given her self-justifying judgment, she cannot fail to believe that pressure to acknowledge her own blameworthiness is coming, independent of her will and wish, from the very person she condemns. By this I do not mean that the accused must actually be resisting and maintaining justifiability. I mean that as part of the self-justifier's action she attributes a condemnatory attitude to the person she accuses.

It works this way. The self-justifier claims that she has a right to act as she is acting toward the person she accuses, *and* that she has this right precisely because he has no right to act as he is acting toward her. This we have already discussed. She regards him as transgressing her rights by overstepping his. And she does not consider his doing so a matter of ignorance or naivete on his part, for if she did she could scarcely be blaming him as she is. She thinks he believes her unworthy of better treatment, not possessed of the right to act as she is acting, inferior in status to himself. So as part of her self-justifying action she believes the person she is condemning is reciprocally condemning her: to perform such an act is to adopt an outlook in which others are one's moral rivals and one is required to defend oneself or face a defeat involving an abject capitulation that might best be thought of as a kind of moral extinction.

I have argued that the self-justifier raises in her own mind the troublesome possibility of her own condemnability in and by the very act of denying it. Hers is a self-troubling act. And this is so because, as we have seen, *what she is defensive about and resistant to admitting—what can seem to observers to motivate her over-elaborate protestations of innocence—is not a possibility apprehended prior to or even independently of her denial of it, but is an aspect of that very act of denial.* Nor does it depend upon anyone actually bringing an accusation against her, and that is why her act appears to anticipate such accusations; it is resistant essentially and continuously rather than just contingently and occasionally. *So as long as she continues to make her claim—which is to say, so long as she maintains the emotional outlook by which she makes it—she is, by definition, resisting 'admission' of a deeply troubling possibility that might look to some like a hidden and suspected truth but is not.*

The material that the self-deceiver denies in maintaining her false conviction, namely, that she is morally condemnable, does serve to motivate her denial—it is the occasion for her self-deception, just as the Standard Theory says. But contrary to the Standard Theory, this motivation is *internal* to the self-deceptive action, in the sense of being the product or concomitant of that action, *and just as false as the conviction that belies it.* Thus the self-justifier insists upon her moral worthiness in acting as she is acting, and feels she *must* insist upon it in order to defeat all suggestion that she might be morally unworthy. That this occasion for her self-deception, this motivation for her denial, is not external to the act it motivates (the self-justifying judgment) in the sense of obtaining independently of it, does not compromise its status as a motivation, for as we have seen the self-justifier *experiences it as external*, as obtaining independently of her will and even her wish, and this is all that is required. Her maintenance of her self-deceived conviction is resistant without consisting in the psychological process postulated by the Standard Theory, namely, the process that begins in a condition in which she believes something straightforwardly (unselfdeceivedly) and is motivated to deny it (because, e.g. of the painfulness, in prospect, of admitting it to herself), and ends in a condition in which she succeeds in this denial, espousing a belief that belies the belief she denies.

SURREALITY

I have argued that what the self-deceiver denies is not a belief she has independently of her denial of it. Her intimation or suspicion or fear that she might be feigning is as false as her claim to be sincere, and the perpetual complement of that claim. Thus her self-justifying action brings into being not simply a false interpretation of itself, but a complement of rival interpretations of itself, both of which are false. It is this 'horizon' of possibilities taken together that is the content of her self-deception. To put this in another way: her self-deception is a falsification of the world, not just a falsification of a particular state of affairs within the world.

It follows that the self-deceiver's claim does not merely fail to be true. It fails to be false also, at least in the normal, opposite-of-true sense of 'false.' For it is false presuppositionally—false in its presupposition that it is capable of being naturalistically produced. The self-justifier's offended affections are not produced naturalistically, and neither are they pretensions, which is the only alternative if they were capable of being naturalistically produced. She is neither sincere nor malingering. What is false, then, is not her claim but what her claim and its negation equally presuppose, namely, that her emotional assessment of her situation is the sort of thing that could be naturalistically produced.

It therefore seems best to say not that the self-justifier's claims are false but that *they have no application to the world*. The moral situation they refer to—including the moral rivalry, the threats to the self-justifier's legitimacy, the need for self-defence, etc.—does not exist; or rather, it does not exist apart from her creation of it by means of her self-deceptive action. In order to discover her self-deception it is not necessary to compare her claims to the world about which she makes those claims, for as I suggested earlier, in discussing the incontrovertibility and vacuity of those claims, they fail not, as she contends, in virtue of anything the accused is doing—not in virtue of the way the world is—but in virtue of her making such claims. Hence her claims are not empirically false; they fail *on principle*.

I want to suggest that what the self-justifier believes that is relevant to her justifiability—and this as we have seen includes much about her circumstances as well as much about herself— is not like an inaccurate portrayal of, say, a garden, which includes representations of toads when in the real garden there are frogs. If this were the character of her beliefs there would be no reason why she could not critically compare this garden to her portrayal of it, see her mistake, and correct the portrayal as necessary. But this is precisely what she cannot do. She is caught between two versions of things, one favourable to her and asserted and one unfavourable and suspected—and *neither* of them accurate. Her rendition of how things are is not so much a portrayal of a real garden but of a fantastical one; not a picture, set in a context of reality, that she might or might not consider critically, but a comprehensive fantastical scenario that she herself inhabits. To abuse Marianne Moore's fond characterization of poetry, it is an imaginary garden with real toads in it, and the self-deceiver, like the poets Ms. Moore wished for, is a 'literalist of the imagination.' The self-deceiver's world is surreal. She is self-deceived not in consequence of some sleight-of-mind by which she manages to trick herself into a false belief, but in consequence of engaging in an action that consists in taking itself and its circumstances to be what, *in virtue of this very action,* they cannot possibly be.[4]

Compare the content of such a self-deceptive scenario to an M. C. Escher drawing, such as "Concave and Convex," "Picture Gallery," "Ascending and Descending," or "Waterfall." Confronting any of the individuals Escher places within the world of the drawing are various possibilities (e.g., to walk a continuously descending staircase that eventually leads back to the starting point). But that world itself is impossible. Just so, confronting self-deceivers are complementary possibilities—the possibility of being morally justified and the possibility of being morally condemnable—where the entire complement is not possible.

THE STRONGEST POSSIBLE FORM OF INTELLECTUAL SELF-ENTRAPMENT

I have tried to show that, by engaging in a self-justifying action, the agent makes a judgment that is both false and, in her mind, decisively supported by what she takes to be the evidence available to her. Insofar as she considers this evidence she finds reinforcement for her conviction. She is trapped intellectually. Engaging in the action is not compossible with understanding it, and the relevant features of the situation, straightforwardly. But this characteristic of self-justifying action does not by itself make it a self-deception. For the intellectual entrapment persists only so long as she maintains her self-justifying judgment. The

---

4 All this ensures that the self-justifier will maintain views that upon close examination are likely to strike an observer as not simply false but mad. For example, in her eyes the person she is accusing cannot possibly be experiencing the sort of emotion she is experiencing. If she is angry him, he cannot in the same sense be angry with her. For believing him responsible for her anger is believing that he can desist from what he is doing if he but will; but if he were experiencing what she is experiencing then by her own account of what she is experiencing he cannot desist. Hence he cannot be experiencing it. Were she to concede otherwise she would thereby be relinquishing her own anger. In her world, no reciprocal anger is possible, as long as she is one of the reciprocators. And if there were reciprocal anger, then both would be warranted and unwarranted at once.

incompossibility of doing this and understanding what she is doing does not explain *why* she persists in doing it. Without a motivation for persisting, an individual would not be intractable in her resistance, as self-deceivers are.

The aspects of the action that make it (anticipatorily) resistant to criticism explain why she persists. As we have seen, engaging in the action provides her with a motivation to continue in it—provides her with a threat against which she feels she must defend herself.

Gabrielle Stolzenberg has formulated what he considers a rigorous set of conditions for intellectual self-entrapment.[5] By his own admission this set needs strengthening, but he himself stops short of strengthening it. The conditions he formulates are

1. Some belief in a system of beliefs is demonstrably false.
2. The procedures that holders of the belief accept as legitimate for questioning the beliefs are all given within the system.
3. None of these procedures undoes this belief.

Clearly a self-justifying action meets these conditions. But the conditions are not sufficient for self-deception. Under them a person could accept a belief and nevertheless be dissuaded from continuing to hold to the entire system of beliefs. No motivation for holding to this system is *systematically* provided, which is to say, no such motivation that is internally related to holding the belief-system. Unless Stolzenberg's conditions are suitably augmented, they contemplate no motivation for holding to the belief-system except those contingently or externally related to the system itself: and this of course means that the motivation might change and leave the individual open to re-

---

5 See his "Can an Inquiry Into the Foundations of Mathematics Tell Us Anything Interesting About Mind?" in George A. Miller and Elizabeth Lenneberg, eds., *The Psychology and Biology of Language and Thought: Essays in Honour of Eric Lenneberg* (New York: Academic Press, 1978) pp. 221-69

consider her doxastic commitments at any time. Soltzenberg is aware of this problem, for in providing an informal restatement of his conditions of self-entrapment he says that "One must be attached to these beliefs so that one will not give them up unless compelled to do so." But this statement is not a formulation of the condition needed to close the loophole. It is an expression (and not a clear one) of the need for such a formulation. In a footnote Stolzenberg comes very near to stating the missing condition: "However, I do not say that the desire to hold these beliefs precedes the state of believing; on the contrary for some beliefs, it may be that the very holding of them produces the desire to hang onto them." Here he is calling for a motivation internally related to the holding of the beliefs in question. Yet he is unable to identify features of any act of holding such beliefs that fulfil his requirement. He knows he needs the following condition but doesn't see how it can be met:

> 4. Holding to this system of beliefs produces the mo-
> tivation to continue holding it—a motivation that is
> 'stronger than'—that systematically distorts and sub-
> ordinates—any motivation to relinquish it.

Self-justifying action possesses the feature required by Condition 4. The motivation, provided within the outlook of the self-deceiver, to defend her claims is the belief she has ineluctably—as part of making the claim—that otherwise she will be acquiescing to a condemnation of herself as a person. To keep insisting upon her justifiability is, given the fact that she is making these claims, the only means available to her of meeting the desperate need she feels, as part of so insisting, to avoid this fate. And since making these claims entails maintaining an entire system of beliefs presupposed by the claims, the motivation for maintaining that system is effectively provided by the system. And finally, it is also provided by the system that her motivations for defending her claim and thus holding to the system will systematically distort and subordinate motivations for reconsidering it, because any motivation to reconsider it, such as contrary evidence or others' disapprobation, will be seen by her as pressing for her condemnation of herself and hence only succeed in reinforcing her motivation to do just the opposite, i.e., to intensify her commitment to the claim.

The analysis I have given has allowed for a peculiarity of self-deception that we meet up with in experience, namely, that people do escape from it. There is serious question whether the two other basic types of self-deception theory, Freud's and Sartre's, can accommodate this fact; they explain the possibility for self-deception by appeal to conditions that make it inevitable—which is to say, that make being free of self-deception impossible. In Freud these conditions consist of structure features of the psyche as it develops in the environmental and social conditions necessary for civilized life, and in Sartre they consist of features of every possible act of consciousness. But the account I am giving identifies self-deception neither with features of the psyche as such nor with features of action as such, but with features of a certain kind of action, self-justifying action; hence, self-deception is by no means ineluctable, since one might not engage in an action of that kind. Though trapped in her self-deception, the self-deceiver is only self-trapped; her motivation for holding her system of beliefs is internal to the system she actively holds. The possibility is open that she can abandon her self-justifying action and relax her allegiance to her system of self-deceived beliefs. What is not open is that she will have a prior motivation for doing so.[6]

But I hesitate to include among the observable features

---

6 How one can escape self-deception and the troubled emotions that attend it when such a motivation is inaccessible I consider *the* central question where the possibility of psychotherapy is concerned. Contemporary psychotherapies are structured to appeal to motivations accessible to the self-deceived and troubled individual—motivations one has in the troubled state for getting out of that state. I believe it follows from the analysis I am offering in this paper that acting upon such motivations only enmeshes the one who does it in the self-deception trap and, I would contend, undercuts their healing potential for that very reason. Clearly this is a question that needs urgently to be addressed.

of self-deceptive conduct *my* observation that people do escape it. Observers with widely differing views of how self-deception is possible might all identify a central core of cases as self-deceptions while disagreeing on others; some might even see self-deceptions in every case. So I refrain from including this as a fourth condition of self-deception. But I can defensibly insist that any theory that entails the impossibility of being free of self-deception is unwarrantedly strong; it precludes possibilities not clearly precluded by any observations. So I take it to be a virtue of my analysis that it avoids doing this.

At the same time, though my account allows for the possibility of escaping self-deception, it does not, strictly speaking, say *how* self-deception is possible in the first place. For though I have shown, I think, that self-deception is possible when it takes the form of self-justifying action, which consists in adopting and maintaining certain accusing and self-justifying and self-presentational emotions, I have not shown how self-justifying action is possible. I have at most offered only an oblique argument. The primary problem with the idea of a self-justifying action seems to be how it is possible without being a cynical, manipulative charade. To Goffman's massive collection of observations of just such self-presenting and self-justifying actions, this has been a repeated criticism; and the clincher in the critics' argument is that since most people aren't cynically manipulative in their everyday interactions, they cannot be managing impressions of themselves in the way Goffman describes. The argument of this paper defeats that criticism; we can now say that self-justifying action as I have characterized it and as Goffman has observed it is not cynically manipulative but is self-deceived. So the obstacle to accepting such observations as Goffman's, and our own confirmations of them, has been removed; self-justifying actions are commonplace, and that of course means that they are possible.

But this seems to me an only slightly more comforting

assurance than what we supposedly already knew—that self-deception itself is possible because it happens. The question is, *How* is self-justifying action, and hence self-deception, possible? Are we sure that the explanation will not introduce anterior beliefs that would undermine its possibility, in the way that self-deception, as standardly conceived, is undermined by the beliefs upon which the self-deceiver is said to act when she deceives herself and resists exposure of her self-deception? This is an issue for another occasion.

IV

THE SOCIAL CONSTRUCTION OF BASIC MISCONCEPTIONS OF BEHAVIOUR

One form of 'individualism' consists in regarding persons as if they were complex objects (things). Associated with individualism in this sense is the idea that the behaviour of these objects is to be explained in terms of causes. In the prevailing contemporary picture the most proximate of these causes are the individual's states and dispositions, so that whatever causal influence the environment has upon the individual is mediated by his or her internal structure and operations. In this scenario, which some social psychologists call 'psychologistic', the social totality or collective plays no part as such; all that transpires may be represented as interactions of the environment and the complex natural objects we call 'persons'. The collective can be said to play a role only in the form of other individuals considered part of one another's environments. The possibility of a social psychology distinctive from this psychologistic scenario depends, it seems to me, upon (a) discreditation of the scenario, and (b) a new conception of the role of the collective in individuals' actions—a conception that avoids anthropomorphizing the collective by treating it as a supervenient person. I think some social constructionists have taken us part way toward such a conception. I think too that when the conception has been developed sufficiently we shall see how it can itself help us discredit the scenario by explaining in social terms why psychologism is both unnecessary and seductive.

But can the twin presumptions of individualism and causalism be discredited? Ought social psychology to emerge as a distinctive discipline, or as *the* psychological discipline? I say Yes to both questions, because I am convinced that these presumptions are aspects of a socially sustained self-deceptive outlook. If I'm right, an adequate social psychological theory should obviously be considered a rival of individualistic psychology, but at the same time it should also be recognized that the struggle between the two, if indeed it ever materializes, cannot be a fair fight. For as we'll see, the basic presumptions of psychologism are presuppositions of a great deal of human behaviour; we very often presuppose them in the way we account for and justify our actions. (In this respect we are all of us self-deceiving.) Hence we're committed to individualism in advance of any psychological inquiry. And it will take more than rational assessment and education to exorcise it; it will require the obliteration of a certain pervasive social practice—almost, the obliteration of a certain form of life.

Self-Justifying Conduct

The following short recollection is typical of hundreds of personal accounts I've collected in the course of my work. A man named Tad wrote that in an extended period around his twelfth year the following conversation, with minor variations, was frequently reproduced in his family, which was part of an ethnic community in a large American city. The style of altercation here is characteristic of much of the United States; members of other cultures learn different ways of accusing others, making themselves out to be victimized, and thereby exonerating themselves.

"What's wrong, Tad?" my mother would ask. "Didn't
  you have a good day?"
"Whadda you care?"
"Son, if you need to talk about your problems, I'd be
  glad to listen."
"Keep yer nose outta my business."
Once we got this far, my father would jump into the
  conversation. What my mother and I had said
  was like priming the pump. It aggravated him
  even more than my sister's humming a tune
  when he tried to give one of his speeches to the
  family on all the things they were doing wrong.
"That's no way to talk to your mother. Even dogs treat
  their own better than that."
"There, there, Dear," Mother would counsel him. "Remember, it's hard to be growing up nowadays."
"It's no favour to him to be allowing this insolence. We
  haven't done anything to deserve it."
"Nuthin', huh? Then why d'ya pick on me all the time?"

Then mother would put her arms around me. "It must be awful to feel nobody likes you." That was the booster blast that would send Dad into orbit.

"I swear you're absolutely ruining him, Blanche. We've sacrificed to give him more opportunities than we gave any of the other children."

"Yeh, just to keep me outta your hair."

"The trouble with you, fella, is you're spoiled. You can't even keep your room straight. Shows just how appreciative you are! The doghouse is cleaner."

"That's where you'd like me to live, isn't it?"

"I've had about all I'm going to take from you."

"Roger, he's only a boy."

"You better shut up, Blanche. Don't start acting like I'm the one who's doing wrong here." My mother's chin would start to quiver, and tears would come to her eyes. This would absolutely infuriate my father. "Don't you dare start crying!" When he'd say that she acted even more wounded than before and she'd bite her lip and the tears would spill onto her cheeks and you could see how hard she was trying not to break down. I almost never heard her retaliate in words. And then he'd turn on me: "You see what you do! You act bad and then when I try to straighten you out she makes it seem like it's all my fault."

"I'm just a spoiled and messy snot-nosed kid, just like you say."

"That's the stupidest thing I've ever heard."

"Ya see! And stupid too." Now I would start to cry, real broken-hearted tears. Mom would be so upset she wouldn't say a word all evening. Dad would be shaking with rage. Some nights I would try to go to sleep so if they came up to my room to check on me they couldn't apologize. One night they came up and couldn't find me. They called out the neighbours to help them look. I had gone outside with a blanket and made my bed in the doghouse.

By the manner or way in which he or she acted, spoke, responded to the others emotionally, etc., each of these people strove to make it clear that what he or she was doing was justified. Each claimed warrant for it by his or her manner or way of doing it. For example, the manner in which Roger corrected Tad was not straightforward. He did not correct him as a father would whose sole concern was his son's improvement. Instead he did it displaying himself as one who was being driven to do it by Tad's abusive insolence and slovenliness and by Blanche's ruinous indulgences of the boy. How did he display himself thus? He did so by his irritability, his flamboyantly exasperated expressions, and his outraged tone. By these means he made himself out to be a man compensating for his wife's destructive influence. A man straightforwardly correcting his son would not do it in this manner. He would proceed in steps likely to secure the son's improvement, steps that he could carry out in private and without Roger's histrionics. But Roger was engaged in a different sort of project; he was insisting (mostly by non-verbal means) upon the moral or emotional necessity of correcting his son. A project of this latter sort involves taking steps of self-display that are unrequired, inappropriate, ineffective, and indeed counterproductive where the aim is straightforward correction.

The distinction I am making between helping and self-justifyingly displaying oneself as helping can be described in another way. Had Roger been straightforwardly helping Tad, securing the boy's welfare would have been his motivation; it would have been the impetus or purpose behind what he did. For a self-justifying person like Roger, securing the boy's welfare played a different role; it was his motivation in a very different sense. It played the role of an imperative for what he did—a model or norm to be emulated by his self-display. Roger sought to qualify his actions as one of those actions that are prompted by concern for another person. Hence the real purpose or impetus behind Roger's conduct could not have been this sort of concern; instead it had to be a concern to secure his own justification.

We are dealing here with a special kind of action, namely, an action that claims warrant for itself in and by the way it is carried out. It's possible to claim warrant for something one has done independently of this action of claiming warrant; though we appropriately call this self-justification, it is different from the kind of action we are studying, which are actions that claim warrant for themselves. For self-justifications of this peculiar kind I'll reserve the name, *self-justifying actions*. Later I'm going to suggest that such actions are commonplace.

The warrant claim made by means of a self-justifying action is made in earnest; the claimant takes it seriously; she believes it. For the action is not a pretence of making that claim (though it might be pretentious); it is not a doubtful effort to convince oneself or a convictionless protestation. (It might be less misleading to call it a judgment than a claim.) This follows from the very definition of a self-justifying action: because it is an action that proffers an account of *itself*, it does not transpire in stages (e.g., a self-assessment and then a self-presentation), and hence there can be no occasion or opportunity for cynical disingenuity or dissemblance.

But how is this possible? How can one make a claim on behalf of one's own conduct that is not separate from the action for which the claim is made?

I think that upon a satisfactory answer to this question

turns the plausibility of many alleged social phenomena, such as paralinguistically and non-verbally expressed information, or roughly what Erving Goffman called 'information management' and 'the presentation of self.' The standard way of 'saving' these phenomena—and by this I mean conceiving them as earnest rather than cynically manipulative—invokes unconscious processes. For reasons I cannot explore here I think this approach, from Freud through cognitive science, is misconceived, and indeed partakes of the untenable presumptions of individualism and causalism that I'm trying to discredit. I'll reserve for another occasion the account of paralanguage and self-presentation that explains how people can be presenting themselves and manipulating others without setting out to do so, but simply in the process of trying to cope with these others as best they can.

CAUSAL PRESUMPTIONS AND 'VICTIMIZED' EMOTIONS

People engaged in self-justifying actions present and take themselves to be defending something they value against a threat posed by someone else. By his demeaning criticisms of Tad, Roger took himself to be anxious to rescue his son's masculinity (the valued object), by teaching him to 'act like a man,' from the damage Blanche was doing. Further, by the deeply offended tones of his rebuke of her, he made it clear how outrageous her insinuation was that he (Roger) was ruining Tad; here the valued item was Roger's own self-respect.

We can make similar observations about Blanche. The claim she made by means of her gestures, expressions, and remarks (by fawning on Tad, by speaking to him piteously, as to one having suffered misfortune, by shielding him physically from Roger, etc.) was something like this: that in coddling Tad she was only trying to overcome the effects of Roger's brutality; that in not expecting Tad to act respectfully she was avoiding blaming him because he was only acting the way he had seen his father act; that she wept only because of Roger's abuse of her; etc. In her mind the threatened goods were Tad's feelings about himself and her personal dignity.

We see then that the content of the self-justifier's warrant-claim is that he is acting defensively—that he is coping with damage someone else is doing or threatening to do and perhaps preventing or compensating for it. In other words, he is judging himself to be a victim. It is not possible to make such a judgment, as opposed to pretending to make such a judgment, without actually experiencing oneself as a victim; whatever he's doing he's having to do only *because* something is being done to him.

This experience of oneself as a victim is a certain kind of emotion or attitude—an accusing emotion or attitude by which another (or others) is judged to be mistreating one, and equally, by which one judges oneself to be a victim. Roger's anger is an example, and so are such emotions and attitudes as rage, fear, sadness, jealousy, envy, pride, despondency, anxiety, hostility, contempt, superiority, and boredom. Actually to make the warrant-claiming judgment is actually to have an emotion of this kind; it is to believe that the person one is accusing is actually causing or threatening to cause some loss, disadvantage, hurt, etc. That Roger regarded Blanche's fussy coddling of Tad as a humiliating critique of all his efforts on the boy's behalf meant that he, Roger, *felt* humiliated in fact. His experience of this emotion was to him the measure of the intensity of the threat he was under and of the value to him of what was threatened. It was evidence of his playing a passive role in the situation—of suffering rather than causing suffering.

Now it is in the very nature of such an accusing, 'victimized' emotion that the person experiencing it cannot believe herself responsible for it. On the contrary, she believes she is being acted upon. If we take seriously the testimony of our experience as self-justifiers, and almost all of us do, we are not responsible for such emotions. The emotion is experienced as being causally produced by the action of the person towards whom the accusation is directed. If Roger is angry with Blanche then he is certain that Blanche is making him angry, and if he were seriously to relax this conviction he would *thereby* abandon his anger. 'Causally produced' here means, 'produced independently of the agent's will or involvement'.

COLLUSION

So far I have emphasized the claims about themselves, their desires, and their emotions made by the members of Tad's family. But these are not the only claims implicit in their self-justifying accounts of themselves. There were also claims about the persons being accused. To maintain that one is defending something valuable from the effects of another individual's conduct is to maintain also that that individual is acting against one's interests. And one must believe these interests legitimate in order to be claiming justification for defending them. So then the claim to be acting purely defensively is a claim that the other person is acting *illegitimately*—immorally, unfairly, or unjustly—in that she is transgressing one's own legitimate rights. This becomes clear when we realize that if, for example, Roger had granted that Blanche was doing little or nothing either to injure Tad or demean him (Roger), then by that very admission he would cease to claim his action defensive, which was an essential part of its point in the first place. So then the claim to be justified that one makes is equally a claim that another is not justified; the two claims are obverses of one another and cannot be separated.

Let us draw out an implication of this point. How would one of the parties in the interchange—Blanche, for instance—have responded if reminded that the other party, Roger, blamed her for Tad's problems? His view was that the very conduct she claimed to be strictly defensive and justified was neither defensive nor justified, but instead unfair or unjust to his interests and therefore *un*justified. To this she would have responded that she did what she did—solicitously looked after Tad, wept in his behalf and her own, etc.—only *because* of the way Roger was treating both of them. What he did gave her what she took to be good reason (motive and justification) for doing what *she* did. Nor is this a judgment she might have made only in retrospect. It was her judgment all along; it was ingredient in her warrant-claims. Though Roger might not like what she was doing, from her viewpoint her having to act as she did could not be laid wholly to her charge. It was Roger who was responsible for having frustrated her legitimate interests as a mother. The same sorts of things can of course be said about Roger.

So the behaviour each took to be defensive, the other considered accusing and provocative. One party's ostensibly defensive measures provided what another took to be good reason (namely, a threat to something valued) for taking defensive measures that provided what the first took to be good reason for taking defensive measures, etc. This situation I'll call *collusion*. Each colluder gives the other ample justification for what the other is doing, and thereby collaborates in it, and does so by actions of taking himself as doing no such thing. (I realize that the word 'collusion' is being used metaphorically; literally the term has come to suggest deliberate and secretive conspiracy, whereas the collaborative conduct I am describing is not deliberately intended to be such. But the only alternative term I can think of is 'psychological symbiosis', and that's quite a mouthful.)

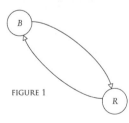

FIGURE 1

For the moment I am going to offer a provisional graphic representation of this situation, even though I shall later argue that no such representation is possible. I do this because the representation will help me construct my later argument and also make a point here (see figure 1).

Now let us try to put Tad into this picture. By his conduct he put forward the claim that his father was abusing him and forcing him out of the family. On the other hand Roger insisted that all his measures were meant to help Tad 'act like a man', take responsibility, etc. But this Tad took to be good reason for his indifference to the condition of his room and for his feeling forced to withdraw; what, he might have asked in his own defence, was he supposed to say, when treated this way? "Thank you, Sir, for pointing out all my shortcomings to me; you are of course correct, so I'll pull myself together right away and try to please you as best I can!"? Is this how he would be expected to respond to humiliating treatment? Certainly not. So Tad responded to his father in the general pattern of his mother, self-pityingly, and this provided what Roger took to be all the more reason to try to straighten Tad out, and all the more cause to blame Blanche. On the other hand, Tad displayed himself as being treated by his mother as incompetent, unable to manage by himself, needing to get away from her interference into every little thing he was doing. So he responded to her in the manner of his father, hostilely, which she took to be all the more reason to pull him back from this pattern of behaviour before it was too late, all the more reason to sorrow because of what Roger was doing to her only son, etc., and all this in turn only fuelled both Tad's and Roger's resolve to persist in their respective courses.

Each party was providing what each other party took to be good reason for his or her conduct, and did so in two ways: Tad provided Blanche with justification for her coddling (which in turn provided him with justification for his hostility and withdrawal), and Roger with justification for his abusiveness (which also provided Tad with justification). Further, the coddling by his mother (in which he colluded) provided his father with justification for the abusiveness. So in a sense Tad managed to provoke his father through provoking his mother and by this route to elicit from his father the justification that the abusiveness provided. And the abusiveness (in which Tad was thereby colluding) was also providing his mother justification for her coddling. So in a sense Tad managed to provoke his mother through provoking his father and by this route to elicit from her the justification that her coddling provided. Extending our graphic representation of collusion, we might depict the whole affair thus:

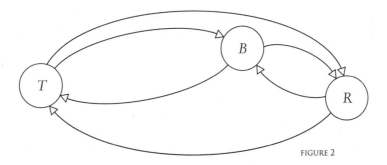

FIGURE 2

The verbal and graphic representations I have made are simplistic, but the general idea should be clear enough. Any number greater than one can play this game; and indeed one (but only one) reason why the survey account I am giving is simplistic is that I am leaving out of it the participation of others—e.g., Tad's siblings and grandparents and the family's neighbours—who may use and be used by any or all of the three people mentioned in Tad's story.

OFFENSE - TAKING

If I claim another person is unjustified because he is acting inimically to something I value, I am thereby claiming he is doing something he has no right to do. And more specifically, I am claiming he is overstepping his rights by violating mine: he is depriving me or threatening to deprive me of my right to possess, enjoy, or protect some particular thing that I value. So unavoidably my claim to be acting defensively involves an appeal to and an insistence upon my own rights and in this respect an insistence that there are certain limits to the rights of the person I am accusing.

An equivalent way to express this same idea is to say that I am claiming to enjoy a certain status as a person, namely, one who possesses the rights in question, and that the way I am being treated by the individual I am accusing does not befit my status. Thus, to put forward a warrant claim for my conduct in and by this self-same conduct is to put forward a warrant claim for *myself*; it is to claim that I am a legitimate, acceptable, or worthy kind of person. Hence the unjustifiability of the person I am accusing consists in his violation of me as a person; it is in virtue of his mistreatment of me that he shows himself not to be the kind of person he claims to be. If he is violating my rights then *a fortiori* I *have* those rights; hence, accusing him of abusing my rights to be treated in such and such a way is a mode or manner of claiming to be the kind of person who possesses such rights.

Let's go back to our story for an illustration of this. From Roger's point of view, Blanche was not merely making herself out to be a proper wife and loving mother. Her 'delicate' and 'tactful' efforts to tone him down and blunt his influence on Tad struck him as accusing him of insensitivity and intolerable harshness; he perceived her whimpering indulgence of Tad and her tears to be overplayed attempts to subordinate him to her control and shame him into changing as a person. It was as if the way she acted was a constant criticism of him. But he was no puppet; he was a 'man's man' and he wanted his son to be a 'man's man' as well, and the more she tried to manipulate him the more out of order he took her to be. To see her as acting illegitimately was thus the same as regarding himself as having a status she was not respecting: her illegitimacy and his legitimacy were in his mind inextricably tied to one another.

Let us take this analysis one step further. Suppose I regard the conduct of my partner in collusion as threatening to *me*—to my concept of myself as a legitimate kind of person. Specifically how does that conduct threaten me? By hypothesis, it is a mirror image of my own; it claims that I am illegitimate in just the sort of way I claim that she is illegitimate. But this alone will not threaten me as a person unless I actually regard her as accusing me of this illegitimacy. So, given that I feel thus threatened in my claim to be a legitimate kind of person—and we have just seen that this must be the case—I *must* be regarding her as attacking my legitimacy. Blanche's moral unacceptability—her disqualification as the kind of person she was actively claiming to be—consisted for Roger in *her* seeing him as morally unacceptable and inferior as a person. In other words, his act of claiming justification for himself consisted in his regarding her as illegitimately regarding him as violating her rights.

Let us represent these findings by a revision of the collusion representation.

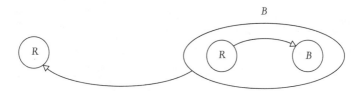

Roger's view of the threat Blanche presents to him

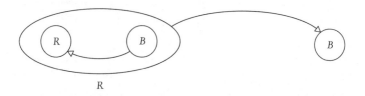

Blanche's view of the threat Roger presents to her

FIGURE 3

Roger presented himself as motivated in part by what Blanche was doing to Tad. But in fact this was only how he presented himself and not what he was doing. What he was doing was presenting himself as the kind of person who was thus motivated. The motivation, in other words, was part of Roger's picture of himself, not a psychological impetus for painting that picture. So this picture included Blanche accusing him, by her coddling of Tad and her whimpering, of *not* being thus motivated—of not being the kind of person portrayed in the picture. Thus it is that by his warrant-claim the self-justifier constitutes another as his accuser.

THE FALSITY OF THE PSYCHOLOGISTIC PRESUMPTIONS

On the agent's self-account of the self-justifying action, he straightforwardly values the thing he professes to be protecting. But on the account that must be given of this self-account, *he values instead the threat that as being presented.* He interprets this as a threat to what he professes to value, but in fact it is a threat to the validity of his status-claim. Without this threat, the status-claim collapses; it is the essential constituent of his justification. Were he to relax his judgment that his partner in collusion is judging him to be an illegitimate kind of person, he would by the same stroke abandon his claims for himself.

Let us test the account the self-justifier gives of himself against the account that must be given of his giving of this account.

In daily life the valuation of the threat is almost everywhere apparent. As I noted already, instead of being occupied straightforwardly with the task of protecting the supposedly valued item from the threat, the offense-taker is characteristically preoccupied with the enormity of the threat, brooding over the injustice being perpetrated against him, overstating the case in

his favour in a manner that aggravates the other parties, pro-
testing too much his innocence of responsibility or the other
person's guilt with gestures, grimaces, repetitions, tone of voice,
etc. (sometimes completely unsolicitedly), refusing to negotiate
a compromise solution even when it would benefit his interests,
recalling what seem to others irrelevant details of their past conduct in order to reinforce his present case against them—and
to all this devoting a degree of energy and concern that, if he
were straightforwardly wanting to protect his professed interests, would at best be unproductive and probably counterproductive. If the other person shows signs of wanting to withdraw
from the collusion he will typically resist. If Blanche had said,
"I'd rather not fight any more, Roger; you give Tad any sort of
counsel you wish," the chances are he would have taken exception to this; he would have interpreted it as offensive. He might
for example have thought or said, "So, you make a mess of him
and then leave me to try to straighten him out by myself!" We've
all seen people who will pout or criticize or complain until finally someone responds negatively, and then they are confirmed
in their conviction that they are being unfairly treated. They
pounce upon the moral shortfall they induce in others as if they
had been dealt a winning card. Thus Tad: "Ya see! And [you
think] I'm stupid too!" I will call this phenomenon, *resistance to
the demise (or withdrawal) of the threat or provocation.* It is a morbid
fixation on the injustice one is suffering or might soon suffer,
and on the culpability of the perpetrator of this injustice. One
does not let go of the threat to one's interests because insisting
that they are being threatened is precisely what one is doing; it is
the substance of the warrant-claim.

A manifestation of this resistance is a kind of irration-
ality we observe in everyday life. People often choose against
what they earnestly claim to be their own best interests and even
sabotage these interests by the way they treat the people they
accuse. Certainly Blanche, Roger, and Tad are examples of this;

they collaborated with what seems an almost professional efficiency in producing a sulking, resentful personality in Tad that each could blame on the others. People do this sort of thing because the loss of what they believe they hold valuable is public proof of the other person's culpability and hence an exoneration of themselves. I have collected many cases in which individuals have in this manner undermined some dream or other to which they were devoting their lives—e.g., a business project, a child, a career path, a relationship—and were able to say in consequence that they could have and would have achieved the dream if only they had not been victimized by forces beyond their control—incompetent employees, a vindictive supervisor, a faithless friend, etc. Thus by a curious illogic they take their suffering as proof of being the kind of person who on his own deserved and would have realized the dream, if he had not fallen among incompetents, petty revenge-takers, mutineers, or thieves. *Any* professed interest is available for sacrifice under the right conditions.

So here we have a reason why the self-justifier's self-account, and specifically the causal presumption in it, is false. If that account were true, the individual would act as efficiently as he could either to flee or to terminate the threat to what he says he values. He would welcome a chance to end the hostilities. He would be willing to let inconsequential insinuations go past, in favour of doing what he could to protect his interests. But we have seen that this is precisely what he does not do and *cannot* do, since in being engaged in his self-justifying action he is insisting on, fixating on, exploiting, etc. this threat: he cannot flee, terminate, or let go of the threat because what he is doing is precisely *not* letting it go. So in this respect too his self-account is not true of his conduct.

Again, if the self-account were true he would be taking the straightforward steps necessary to protect his interests, but this is just what he does not do. Roger could have taken Tad aside, befriended him, taught him patiently what he wanted him to learn, asked him 'please,' etc.—in short dealt with him in the sort of manner that he himself would have found acceptable. Proceeding thus was an opportunity embarrassingly obvious, and anyone with reasonable intelligence would be able to see it immediately—provided his whole interest was to instruct and correct the boy. What Roger in fact did was dictated by another sort of aim altogether, namely, claiming the necessity of correcting Tad, and that meant publicly emphasizing Tad's deficiencies and Blanche's destructiveness in a manner that demotivated both of them, but showed whoever would believe him what perverse and recalcitrant people he was forced to work with.

THE INTERCONSTITUTIVITY OF THE COLLUDERS' ACTIONS; THE FALSITY OF THE INDIVIDUALISTIC PRESUMPTION

I want briefly now to take up what I will call the individualistic presumption in the self-justifier's self-account. I mean by this the idea that what each colluder is doing is independent of what the others are doing and determinate in its own right. Clearly this presumption is present in the self-accounts that colluders offer. Refer for a moment to Figure 3, which is the depiction of the situation from the individual colluder's point of view. The possessor of this point of view does believe his "emotional state" (which is in fact a part of what he is doing) is being produced by another person, but what he takes to be his action is another matter. In being engaged in it, he believes himself to be making an independent choice whether overtly to express his frustration, irritation, anger, disappointment, humiliation, contempt, or whatever, and deal with his colluder in the way he deserves, or to control his inclination to express himself 'in spite of' the mistreatment he is suffering.[1] His view is that the other person is acting wholly without complicity from him, maliciously or inconsiderately mistreating him, and cynically pretending not to be. For the colluder, then, the clear-cut action of each of the participants (as distinguished from his own motivation) is instigated and carried out autonomously by the agent himself.

Though I haven't space to discuss at length the reasons why this individualistic presumption is false, I will state three of these reasons very broadly. (I) Take two colluders, Blanche and Roger. Blanche's responses are constituents of what Roger is doing, and conversely. We have already seen that *his account* of what she is doing is a constituent of *his account* of what he himself is doing. But my thesis is stronger than this: it is that *her act of giving her account* is a constituent of *his act of giving his account*. It works roughly like this. In his point of view, her claims on her own behalf, which he saw her as making, were condemnatory of him. She cried and whimpered; outraged by this ludicrous condemnation of him, he said something like this: "Don't you dare start playing the victim." But perhaps she might one day have said something very different—something he did not anticipate—e.g., the sort of possibility we noted earlier: "I'm not going to do battle with you over Tad any more, Roger; you deal with him however you want." Roger would not have been at a loss to manage this manoeuvre, however uncharacteristic it might have been. He would (so long as he continued his self-justifying course of conduct) have construed it as an offense. "You make everyone think what's gone wrong with Tad is all my fault and then you self-righteously decide you don't want to talk about it any more!" Or imagine that Blanche might have made this uncharacteristic move: "I've realized you are right, Roger. What

---

1 A possible exception to this may be the case in which the individual presents himself as so intensely provoked or aroused that it is not within his power to make this choice; in thus presenting himself he will not regard himself as acting autonomously, but this may be because he will not regard himself as acting at all-the situation here is a bit blurry. At any rate, there is no such vagueness in his judgment about the other person's autonomy.

Tad needs is a firmer hand of discipline." Unless he suddenly gave up his self-justifying course, Roger would probably have wondered what sort of sinister game Blanche was playing now, or whether she was making fun of him. Or he might have said, "So you've finally got around to admitting you've been the one who's done the damage—after it's too late." Or Blanche might have executed the highly sophisticated manoeuvre of coopting Roger's condemnation of her and castigated herself soundly, falling into despondency over her failures as a wife and mother. It would have been the ultimate form of accusation to insinuate that through their experience together as husband and wife she had lost all faith in herself as a person and all hope for life. In such a case Roger might have been even more exasperated with her, or he might have tried to talk her out of her self-recriminations in order to assuage his own guilt. Thus any move Blanche might have made could have been construed by Roger offendedly; *his interpretation of it would have been the next move HE made. What he did at each stage of the collusion was an appropriation of what she did, and was therefore partly constituted by what she did.* His self-deception was not the individualistic weaving of a solipsistic fantasy but a practice engaged in with others that no individual could possibly have carried on alone. Collusion is not a matter of individual actions taken in turns, but of *corporate* action, to which each participant makes a contribution that cannot be individualistically described.

(2) Entailed by the individualistic presumption is the idea that what each colluder does, considered independently from what the others are doing, is determinate. Blanche believed she had the determinate intention to cope defensively as best she could with Roger's abusiveness, and no intention to disregard his legitimate interests or to put him down. And she believed that he had a determinate intention to pursue his interests at her expense. But *there are no such intentions; and I say this because both interpretations—the exonerating one and the condemnatory one—are*

equally false. I say that the intentions ascribed by colluders have no psychological reality as intentions; they have a psychological reality, *if any*, as self-deceived self-displays by which the agent claims to have these self-same intentions. I do not deny that we sometimes formulate intentions explicitly, independently of our carrying them out; I deny only that we formulate them thus in what I am calling self-justifying action.

Remarks like this may meet with incredulity. But what is the intention, we want to ask? What is the individual doing? I am challenging the productivity of questions like this. That they have captured our imagination is not proof that they have answers. Indeed, it may just as well be what we would expect if the account I have been giving in this paper is sound: that we vacuously confirm the applicability of such questions by our experiences because we are self-deceivingly entrapped by those experiences.

I say there is no *individualistically* determinate intention or action where self-justifying action is concerned. The essential negativity of a claim to moral legitimacy makes that claim a spontaneous interpretation of the perhaps unexpected responses of others. Thus what the individual believes he is doing is not pre-formulated, but is whatever he makes of the others' responses to him. For just this reason, namely, that his claims for himself are essentially claims about the other, these claims *cannot be self-contained* but *must* depend upon the other's further response. The account he claims for himself is therefore constantly subject to further determination; his conduct takes on meaning as the situation develops, and then he proceeds as if that were what he had all along intended. (This is an approach to what John Shotter, following Peter Ossario, calls an *ex post facto fact*.) All this is compatible with the self-accounting quality of the self-justifying action. I 'aim at' a conception of myself and my conduct; I present myself as being such and such a kind of person, and my action such and such a kind of action. *But this aim is*

an ever-accumulating interpretation of others' ever-accumulating responses.
The wide adaptability of my offendability empowers these others reciprocally to constitute the content of my accusation of
them, which means it empowers *them* to constitute *my* reasons
for my convictions about myself.

(3) Notice that if we take the individualistic interpretation seriously, we cannot assemble a coherent representation of
the collusion. For each possessor of an individualistic picture,
the exterior arrow represents a naturalistic causation, and the
interior arrow a spurious claim of naturalistic causation. We cannot overlay the pictures without an inconsistency. For example,
if we were to overlay them, each colluder would be both warranted and unwarranted. Each would be doing something properly given a description that implies a strictly defensive intent
and yet not doing it. The conviction that the pictures cannot be
amalgamated is a feature of every colluder's self-accounting. If
A is angry with B then it is impossible in his eyes that B is angry
in the same sense, i.e., caused to be angry by A, for if A were
to grant this he would thereby no longer be blaming B for his
response—he would no longer be angry—but would be laying
the responsibility upon himself. Sense can't be made of the individualistic picture.

THE PREVALENCE OF COLLUSION

My contentions in this paper would not be very important if self-justifying action and the collusion in which it is embedded were an infrequent phenomenon. But on the contrary
it appears to be commonplace (though I believe not universal).
For consider what it would mean for someone, say Blanche, not
to be colluding when someone else's offense-taking, say Roger's,
implied condemnation of her. It would mean that she would
see his conduct for what it was, namely, a display of himself as
aggravatedly miserable and a taking of that misery to be evi-

dence of the harm she was doing. It would mean perceiving this conduct for what it was without feeling hurt by it; she would see Roger doing harm to himself rather than to her. She would not see him self-justifyingly but straightforwardly. For reasons I cannot try to explore here, I believe that to see a person self-deceivingly ruining her life for proof of a chimerical moral status (that is, for others' validating accusatory response which is given *only* because giving it is validating for them), and to do so without taking any offense (without feeling injured by what she is doing) is to see her compassionately. I shall suggest in a moment that this point has profound implications for the form that a non-collusive social science might take.

Is this straightforwardness widespread? That is some sort of empirical question, I suppose. It seems to me that all of us experience something akin to it in some sectors of our lives, e.g., when we see an offense-taker involved in a collusion far removed from our own concerns, or when someone accuses us of not measuring up in an area about which we have no insecurity whatever—either because we don't care or because we are not trying to prove anything in that area. But insofar as we are insecure—that is, insofar as we are disposed toward self-justifying conduct—it is at least very unlikely that we would not take offense. I think the analysis I have been offering in this paper applies to most of what we do. And I think one evidence for this is the prevalence of class- or group-consciousness—of what might be called 'kind-of-person-consciousness'—that manifests the mutually alienating moral judgments of colluders. Society as we know it—'moral orders' of persons arranged differentially by status and rights—is communal collusion.

THE SOCIAL CONSTRUCTION OF OUR
MISCONCEPTIONS OF OURSELVES

I am now in a position to make my primary point. Blanche presents Tad and Roger with options of interpretation—not deliberately, but simply in virtue of engaging in her self-justifying conduct. They can either take her side, concurring that she is suffering as she believes she is and that Roger is responsible for this suffering; or they can stand against her and challenge her claim to victimhood. "Whadda you care?" asked Tad of the mother who was sacrificing everything to demonstrate her concern. "Don't you dare start crying!" said Roger about her demonstration that she was responding to forces beyond her control. Anyone who had taken her side-perhaps her mother did—would have vindicated her, but so did these who stood against her, for given the actuality of her suffering they were only showing her, by their opposition, the absurdity of their position. By standing against her they were only continuing to victimize her in just the way she had been accusing them of all along. We can see that anyone who had accepted Blanche's proffered set of options by choosing one of them would have been colluding with her and would *thereby,* have been making with her the causal and individualistic presumptions. *To collude is to conspire with others in taking these ideas as an unexamined background of all judgments; it is tacitly to agree that this will be the basis of agreement that makes moral disagreements possible.*

My main point then is that the generation of the psychologistic conception of what persons are is a social achievement. It is propagated wherever there is social insecurity and the self-justification that manifests this insecurity, and reinforced wherever an insecure person takes offense by it. In this sense the picture of persons thus propagated can be thought of as a construction achieved by colluding persons. The construction proceeds by the induction of individuals into the practice of collusion. Is this only the social construction of an image of what we shall agree are persons, or is it in some sense also the construction of persons themselves? Clearly the image isn't an accurate representation of persons, so in this sense collusion is not the social construction of persons. Yet in another sense it is: the construction is indirectly and partly the construction of persons as creatures who engage in this collaborative construction of false self-images, this corporate act of delusion.

THE MORAL CONDITIONS OF UNDERSTANDING PEOPLE

Is a study of human beings possible that does not partake of this delusion? I believe so, but the conditions are severe. It is possible to observe and objectively represent the activity of a colony of South American honey ants in which each individual ant carries out its task without comprehension of the corporate activity and accomplishment, but with an efficiency and coordination that having this comprehension could scarcely improve. I cannot see that it is possible to do the same for the corporate kind of activity I'm calling collusion, where individuals interpreting their situations individualistically proceed, as if orchestrated, to provide one another with validations for their self-deceptions in corporate actions which none of them comprehends. Every attempt made thus far to formulate such a representation is an extension, a generalisation, or an amalgam of individualistic representations, and none of them is adequate or, I think, even coherent. Indeed the very idea of an objective or dispassionate, yet non-individualistic, representation of collusory action may presume a point of view that is disqualified in advance from understanding its subject matter.

This does not mean understanding is not possible. But to understand, I have suggested, is a matter of compassion. It is a matter of being in or entering into a situation as a moral individual fully engaged, prepared to do whatever his humanity and the humanity of the others would require of him. I do not think one can withhold oneself from this with whatever intent, even to try dispassionately to formulate what's going on, without falsifying the situation, and specifically, without reintroducing the causal and individualistic presuppositions in some form. For withholding oneself thus could only be a stance motivated by some self-justifying interest. Such an interest might be to present oneself as a scientist or a scholar—qualifying to be thought of as 'scientific' or 'scholarly' by some culturally local criterion of professional legitimacy. The idea of putting the humanity of oneself and of others first would under these conditions seem to block the path to legitimacy. One would have to give up proving anything about oneself. Not understanding might be the price we have to pay for a certain kind of 'science'; abandoning the pursuit of that kind of science might be part of a quest for bona fide understanding.

We cannot make parents, managers, teachers, therapists, or doctors effective solely by training them in skills; besides possessing 'know-how' they must also be sensitive, caring, and compassionate. This is not just because they come across poorly when they lack the human qualities; it's equally because they don't see what's there to be seen of the moral reality of other people. So it is with our own efforts to prepare ourselves to understand people-this seems so utterly obvious that I'm amazed I've so often lost sight of it. We are constantly at risk of collaborating in delusion and eclipsing human reality altogether.

V

IRONY, SELF-DECEPTION
AND UNDERSTANDING

A certain kind of moral goodness is necessary for understanding the speech and conduct of others. This proposition isn't quite as hard to square with our intuitions as might first appear. We would all be willing to grant that if we are self-serving, manipulative, and ready to take offense, we will have a heavy investment in interpreting others' conduct to favour ourselves and all else being equal will inevitably do so. But philosophically speaking this observation isn't very interesting. It suggests nothing general about the form the distortion of understanding must take and very little about the sort of morality required to avoid or rectify that kind of distortion. Yet there is an account of the self-deception involved in a self-serving, manipulative, and offense-taking attitude that supplies these lacks. It shows how, when we're self-deceived, our perception of others is deformed systematically, in a predictable pattern. And it suggests something about the peculiar moral quality of any attitude or outlook that is free of this pattern of deformation, which is to say it suggests how self-deception and freedom from it are rooted in the active ongoing constitution of social relationships. Along the way I will briefly suggest that the account of self-deception that provides these conceptual benefits is demonstrably free of the well-known inconsistencies of other accounts.

AN APPARENT DEFICIENCY
OF DESCRIPTIVE DISCOURSE

If what I'm claiming is true, the self-deceiver will misconstrue any adequate description proffered him of whatever it is he's deceiving himself about. If enough people share his self-deceptive outlook, whoever is offering that description may become discouraged about the possibility of making that description univocally. He may begin to think the linguistic resources at his disposal are deficient. Let me illustrate.

Clarissa Marchant was what was once thought of as a 'genteel' lady of the American South, aristocratic, privately educated, musically accomplished, poised, and above the frivolity and vulgar pleasures of most of her contemporaries, including almost all of those who had been in school with her. Yet it was not with the few individuals in the area who shared her tastes that she spent her time socially, but with the very people whose low-life delights she found contemptible. Out of what she experienced as her largesse of soul, she staged delightful occasions 'at home' to which she invited these people. Though they enjoyed being with one another, they seemed as awkward around her as she was aloof from them, in spite of the fact that she and they had all known each other from childhood. On one surprising afternoon a friend paid a call with serious purpose in mind.

HELOISE: Clarissa, I've been wanting to talk with you. About the classical music you play and the paintings and statues you surround yourself with. I think you're, well, stuck up. You think you're better than the rest of us.

CLARISSA: (recomposing herself after this). I'm sorry you feel that way. If I had known that any of the things I enjoy would make you feel uncomfortable, I certainly would not have put them on display. They're not worth that much to me.

HELOISE: Don't patronize me! I've screwed up my courage to come over here and talk to you about this problem you have of being uppity, and you start getting uppity with me! You act as if it's my problem.

CLARISSA: Why Heloise, I'm taken completely off my guard. I don't know what to say.

HELOISE: Of course you don't. Obviously no one has ever pointed out the truth to you before.

CLARISSA: (sitting down). You are saying that I am, well, haughty? Superior in my feelings toward people?

HELOISE: Yes, that's it.

CLARISSA: And that I display music and art in my home to show everyone how superior I am?

HELOISE: That's it exactly.

CLARISSA: But that means I don't really enjoy these things for themselves alone.

HELOISE: Not in the true sense of 'enjoy'.

CLARISSA: Do you think the charitable work I do and the evenings we have together are all a sham too? Am I just pretending when I do those things?

HELOISE: Well not exactly. If you were just pretending it would be play-acting.

CLARISSA: And I'm not play-acting?

HELOISE: Of course not, because play-actors come off the stage sometimes, and I don't think you ever do.

CLARISSA: I'm always acting?

HELOISE: No, no, that's not what I mean. You don't know

you're doing it, so it's not acting.

CLARISSA: You mean, I'm pretending and I don't know I'm doing it?

HELOISE: That's not a good way to say it. You're changing it all around.

CLARISSA: I'm honestly trying to understand. When I play the viola, do I really feel the peace and swelling motions inside of me, or not?

HELOISE: (increasingly frustrated). Well, you feel them, I wasn't saying you didn't really feel them.

CLARISSA: And what about my attitude towards people? That concerns me. Do I care about them or don't I?

HELOISE: It's not that you don't care. It's that you won't mingle. You keep yourself on a higher level than the others. People feel common around you. When we were all dating and rowdying around in school, you were playing in concerts—as if you were too good for us.

CLARISSA: Don't you think some of the things you did were pretty crude?

HELOISE: Well, yes, I do now.

CLARISSA: Did you expect me to compromise myself in order to do what you were doing?

HELOISE: No, of course I didn't expect you to compromise anything, and I don't now.

CLARISSA: Is my assessment of the kind of life most people lead an unrealistic one?

HELOISE: No, I agree with that mostly. Everyone wants to be better than they've been. It's not bad to want to be better. But you, and your children too, you make people feel humiliated.

CLARISSA: Are you quite certain this is my doing? Might it not be something within these people themselves? Perhaps resentment? Or jealousy? Or regret?

HELOISE: I can't deny you're sincere in your own way.

CLARISSA: Let's put an end to this unpleasant conversation and forget we ever had it. Let it be just a ripple that subsides forever. My daughter Stephanie and I would consider it an honour if you and Penny would have lunch with us tomorrow.

Heloise was unable to make her point to Clarissa. When she tried to formulate it, she seemed to say something else entirely. She had wanted to say Clarissa's conduct was demeaning. In Clarissa's mind, this could mean only that it was intentionally demeaning, i. e. malicious and cynically manipulative of others. This was a charge so strong—so different from how Clarissa experienced herself—that it could not be taken seriously. And under Clarissa's pressure Heloise felt forced to acknowledge that making this charge was going too far, as indeed it was. In a variety of ways Clarissa relentlessly insisted she could not be faulted at all without being made out to be a monster; behind this insistence lay the assumption that unintentionally demeaning conduct is impossible. So Clarissa was certain that though her friends may have taken offense, she hadn't given offense. Such was the manoeuvre by which, in her own mind at least, she shook Heloise's confidence in the reasonableness of her complaint. (It is not uncommon to observe manoeuvres like Clarissa's and responses like Heloise's. "I'll thank you to mind your place in the queue," says one. The other says, or perhaps only thinks, "Are you suggesting I'm purposely trying to push past you?")

How is it that Clarissa was able to execute this manoeuvre and neutralize Heloise's accusation so handily? There are two possibilities:

1. Clarissa was right: it is in fact impossible for conduct to be offensive without being malicious. On this possibility, Clarissa neutralized the accusation simply by pointing this out and insisting that her conduct had to be either offensive and

malicious or neither of these.

    2. Clarissa was wrong, and Heloise shouldn't have con-
curred with her. There *can* be attitudes and conduct that are
offensive and not malicious, and Clarissa's were among these.

This second possibility is the possibility that Clarissa
was self-deceived; that is, she was doing something other than
what she was systematically taking herself to be doing, and just
as systematically, was defensive about any interpretation of her
conduct contrary to her own. She was elevating herself in her
own eyes by putting others down, which is not something one
can do while realizing one is doing it, because then one could not
be taking the self-elevation seriously. She experienced herself
as suffering their vulgarity and insensitivity magnanimously and
thus confirmed her self-deceived sense of herself—her sense of
being a person of rare sensibility who is courageously bearing
the burden of isolation that is the price of her gifts. This again is
something that cannot be done in the realization that it is being
done.

    I want to explore this second possibility: that Claris-
sa was self-deceived in her interpretation of herself and consequently in her interpretation of Heloise's complaining description of her. But notice in passing that Clarissa's disallowance
of this possibility is exactly the disallowance made by most who
have written on the possibility of self-deception (though she did
not engage in any of their elaborate reasonings): We cannot
be doing something self-deceivingly without having an explicit
ulterior intention of doing it, which requires in turn that to be
deceiving ourselves about this intention we must be taking note
of it; it must then be with another explicit intention that we
keep ourselves from taking note of our taking note of the first
intention, and so on. So as was pointed out right at the beginning of the contemporary discussion of self-deception, in trying
to account for self-deception, we're caught in either self-contra-

diction or infinite regress.[1] Self-deception thus formulated is impossible, just as intentionally demeaning conduct formulated in Clarissa's way is impossible.

So if there was any substance to Heloise's complaint— if Clarissa had indeed been demeaning without being malicious—then Clarissa could not have been guided by an explicit ulterior intention or strategy. And again, when she managed to draw Heloise into her self-deceived view of herself, as surely she did, she could not have intended to do so, or been guided by an explicit strategy. Otherwise, Clarissa would have been right: what she was charged with would have been impossible—and self-deception generally would also be impossible. If Clarissa was self-deceived, what no doubt seemed to Heloise a manipulative cross-examination had to be like Clarissa's other dealings with her friends: offensive but not malicious, not intentional. So we can let the possibility of Clarissa's self deception hang on this: How could she have so effectively neutralized Heloise's charge against her without explicitly intending to do so, and without being guided by a strategy for doing so?

SELF-DECEPTION

Clarissa's sense of herself in relation to the others was a straightforward response. It arose as a natural response to the objective features of circumstances she was in, without any interposition of intention or purpose on her part. In other words, she believed herself caused by the circumstances to feel as she did.[2] One cannot feel superior to another without believing it is because of one's own qualities in comparison to the qualities of the other, just as one cannot be angry with someone unless one regards that individual as making one angry. Again, one cannot feel isolated and misunderstood without believing it is because

---

1 See Herbert Fingarette, *Self-deception* (London: Routledge & Kegan Paul, 1969).

2 In her mind, it was subsequent, and in response, to this naturalistically determined attitude that her purposes and intentions came into play—namely, to deal with this personally unrewarding situation honourably.

of others' insensitivity, etc.

We might call the attitude and emotions we are discussing *offense-taking attitudes*; for brevity's sake, I'll henceforward use the term 'attitude' to refer to both attitudes and emotions. An offense-taking attitude consists in part of one or more judgments about its own genesis. In Clarissa's case, these might have included such judgements as, "You (Heloise) require me to sacrifice my own projects in order to share my interests with you." And: "You don't appreciate all I'm trying to do for you." And: "If only my tastes weren't so refined I might be able to mingle more freely with your kind." People having an offense-taking attitude are all self-conscious, in the sense that by means of the attitude they make a judgment about the origin of that very attitude; they justify themselves in having that attitude. We might say that to be able to engage in such an attitude is to have acquired a sort of theory about its genesis. To learn when and how to take offense is to learn when and how to impute to situations a naturalistic or causal responsibility for one's offended feelings. I don't mean by this that a theory of such things is deployed independently of taking offense: to say this would make us all much more sophisticated than we are. I mean only that the attitude itself is a bit of theorizing—or at least of explanation, if that sounds better—as to who or what is responsible for that very attitude.

Now consider the theory implicit in Clarissa's attitude, namely that the attitude is being naturalistically or causally produced and that she, Clarissa, is therefore not responsible for any part of it. Given this theory, if at any point she were to have granted that she was responsible for this attitude then she could not have continued to maintain the attitude at all, since it includes a belief that it itself is being naturalistically produced. So in her mind, her attitude was either as she says it was—straightforward on her part—or else she was not experiencing it at all, but only feigning. But in fact she was experiencing it; she was in fact engaging in all the inner conduct—the assessments, criticisms, and defensive rejoinders—in which having such an attitude largely consists. Hence she could not be feigning. So the mere fact of having the attitude constituted for her what she considered proof that she was not responsible for her attitude, and that Heloise was wrong to accuse her. Thus it was that with no strategy or cleverness on her part, with no intention of doing so, Clarissa neutralized Heloise's criticisms merely by taking them seriously against the background of her 'theory'.

So Clarissa achieved her defensive victory without laying a strategy for doing so, and this in virtue of structural properties of that attitude. She could not have adopted the attitude and allowed for the possibility of being self-deceived in it; she could not have allowed for the possibility of being in any way responsible for it.

I suggested already that this same logical narrowmindedness or prejudice has haunted the self-deception literature. Writers on this subject have almost all failed to avoid imputing to the self-deceiver the very belief she is said to be deceiving herself about, and by this imputation they have turned self-deception into ordinary, cynical deception in just the way Clarissa did. They have then been faced with Clarissa's choice: either what's called self-deception is cynical pretence or else it's straightforward. So the widespread doubt about the possibility of self-deception is not surprising. I want to take a step toward overcoming this doubt by pointing out this: The theorists' problematic conception of self-deception is indeed impossible, but what it's a conception of is not self-deception; self-deception is something else. Behind this conception lies the naturalistic error. Self-deception theory is troubled because it partakes of the self-deceiver's outlook.

UNDERSTANDING SELF-DECEPTION

Now that it's reasonably safe to proceed on the assumption that Clarissa might indeed have been self-deceived, we can turn to the central question: How are we to describe self-deceptive attitudes and conduct without buying into the theory implicit in them, which is Heloise's error. Heloise colluded in Clarissa's evasion by capitulating to Clarissa's theory. Our task is to describe self-deception without colluding in it.

An obvious first ploy is to try to devise a special vocabulary. But suppose we introduce new descriptors for Clarissa's self-deception. Being self-deceived, she not only can but inevitably will apply these terms to herself in precisely the same evasive fashion as she applied the old ones, and by this means will preclude what we want to mean by them. So the new vocabulary will change nothing; with it Clarissa can induce collusion as easily as before.

In desperation we might try to utilize the existing vocabulary to get round what I called 'Clarissa's choice' and say something other than either of Clarissa's false interpretations. We might try to do this with an oxymoron such as 'Clarissa's condescending refinement.' I think Sartre uses this tactic repeatedly for a similar subject matter in *Being and Nothingness*, most obviously when he refers to the being "that is what it is not and is not what it is." This won't work because *from the self-deceiver's point of view* it implicitly endorses his supposition that the options in the situation are limited to two: condescension, which is cynical, and refinement, which is not. The oxymoron may serve *us* who understand why it was devised, as long as we keep in mind that we are trying to say there is something going on here other than both cynicism and sincerity. But it won't satisfy Clarissa or prevent Heloise from colluding with her. It can't bear the descriptive load by itself. If Heloise insists Clarissa is condescending, then she can't be speaking literally when she says she's refined, and if Clarissa can establish that she's not condescending in any intentional way, she can confirm in her own mind her conviction that her refinement is genuine.

Let us then abandon these attempts to augment our lexical resources artificially and consider whether they might be adequate just as they are. To do this we must consider what Heloise might be contributing to the appearance of their inadequacy. She was not wholly Clarissa's dupe, but, as one of Clarissa's colluders, was herself self-deceiving; she was collaborating in setting up the false alternatives of interpretation I have up to now ascribed solely to Clarissa. For it is clear that Heloise's concerns and motivations were very much like Clarissa's in all the respects relevant to the sort of self-deception we are discussing. Self-vindication was just as important to her. Exonerating herself by taking offense—by viewing others as transgressing against her—was as much her pattern as it was Clarissa's. When Clarissa treated her as an inferior, she construed the charge implicit in that treatment in much the same way that Clarissa construed Heloise's charge of haughtiness. To Heloise it meant either that she was a vulgar kind of person and the worse for the fact that she could do something about it if she but would, or that she was perfectly innocent. Since the first alternative didn't fit at all with her experience of herself, the second one had to be right, and Clarissa had to be profoundly out of order in a moral way to treat her as she had. So Heloise was an active collaborator in the delimitations of interpretation imposed upon her remarks to Clarissa. And that means in order to test whether the language is adequate, in and of itself, for saying what was going on with Clarissa, we must imagine what it would be like not to recapitulate Heloise's collaboration, or in other words, to be free of her self-serving, manipulative, and offense-taking attitude.

I should like to conduct this exercise of imagination by means of a parable. Imagine a cadre of visitants to our society. Call them 'angels.' The angels are guileless; they have no investment, as Heloise did, in how the conduct of others is to be understood. One of them, Bertha, has Clarissa on her visitation list. Of her she must periodically report after making careful observations. During her visits she frequently hears Clarissa speaking in her mind (angels can do this) of the extent of her suffering and her noble handling of it. Bertha watches her in many situations—with Heloise and the others, playing her viola, at the museum board meetings, writing in her diary. When she returns to headquarters she updates her superiors about Clarissa and reports that "Clarissa is suffering, yet proud of the way she is managing." And everyone present understands about Clarissa.

Why? Because they know about Clarissa. They know she's steeped in self-concern and self-exoneration; they know she nurses the thoughts of others' social shortcomings and finds a satisfying consolation in the loneliness that comes of being free of those shortcomings. Hence they understand directly that her suffering is not the straightforward, wholly inflicted thing she makes it out to be. Nevertheless, it is suffering, since it is actually undergone and not merely feigned. Similar remarks could be made about Clarissa's pride. To Bertha and any other non-colluder with a normal range of emotional experience, all this is obvious. "She's suffering yet proud of how she's managing" describes Clarissa's condition perfectly well. The language is descriptively adequate. It is not the language or Bertha's use of it, but the self-deceived interpretation of Clarissa and her colluders, that introduces inadequacy.

In his paper "The Man Who Mistook His Wife For a Hat,"[3] the neurologist Oliver Sacks described one Dr P., a musician and music teacher suffering from visual agnosia; he had lost the capacity to recognize everyday objects, including people, though he could identify their individual features perfectly well. If he could mnemonically associate some unique and prominent feature of the object with his notion of that object then he could

3 Oliver Sacks, *The Man Who Mistook His Wife for a Hat* (London: Pan Books, Ltd., 1986)

make the identification inferentially, but this was different from seeing what it was—for example, simply seeing that this particular object was his wife's head (rather than his hat), or that that particular object, which he identified as a "continuous surface infolded on itself. . .with five outpouchings," was a glove. Nor could he grasp the whole of a scene or utilize it as context for identifying the items in it; he could recognize only isolated or abstracted bits. He could get parts, concrete and abstract, and could to a certain degree assemble them by using a rule explicitly, but visually (not auditorily) he lacked a sense of the physiognomy of wholes. The mnemonic features that served him best were musical or quasi-musical ones, such as characteristic movements; he had a much better chance of inferentially recognizing someone if he observed that person's characteristic 'body-music' than if he were presented only with static features. It was almost as if he had been reduced to operating in an atypical and limited cognitive key, and captured what experience he could in that key.

I wonder whether agnosia is not an apt metaphor for self-deception—a metaphor only, rather than a diagnosis, because the self-deceiver's degenerate sense of totalities is not due to an affliction he suffers, but is something he brings upon himself. I am not speaking here of the fact that the self-deceiver does not recognize individuals for what they are, in their own terms, but sees them, abstractly, as either threats or allies in the face of threats. I am speaking instead of his (perhaps temporary) inability to grasp the physiognomic totality of what is going on—he has no sense of the form of the social action in which he is participating; he apprehends only simplistic and stylized aspects of the situation. (If we turn the musical perception metaphor completely around we might say: It's almost as if his rendition of reality were made without benefit of the key signature; it's as if he played the scales without sharps or flats. It's possible to attempt a transposition of social music under such conditions, but not without the characteristic losses and deformations I have been talking about in this paper.) In the rest of this paper I will explore further what it means to say that the self-deceiver lacks this sense.

Through a series of events Bertha's report is challenged. She is called to an inquest. Present are some of Bertha's own cadre and also a number of other individuals who do not share her guilelessness. All of these latter have colluded in Clarissa's self-deception, some as her defenders and some as her accusers.

JUDGE: The transcript states that you said Clarissa has been suffering yet is proud of the way she is managing in spite of this. Is that correct?

BERTHA: Yes, Your Honour.

JUDGE: Will you stand by that report, or do you want to amend it?

BERTHA: I stand by it.

The courtroom is in commotion. Clarissa's defenders are claiming victory. Bertha's testimony, they are sure, has established Clarissa's sincerity. Her accusers are screaming that nothing definitive has been shown. It is plain to them that Clarissa's display of so-called suffering, as they describe it, is in fact self-concern, and not the sort of anxiety that springs from a pure concern for others' welfare.

The judge quiets the courtroom and, drying her brow with her handkerchief, asks whether Bertha might settle the dispute with a suitable explanation of her intent. After reflecting intensely, but only momentarily, Bertha simply answers, "No."

From several millennia of service Bertha has learned that any qualification she might make of her report will inevitably be misunderstood by those who are colluding with Clarissa, just as her initial report was misunderstood. She will be taken to say either that Clarissa was sincere and a victim or that she was playing the martyr in order to get away with the reprehensible thing she was doing. Bertha understands that there is nothing more she can say.

Both Bertha's position and attitude at this moment are ironic. It is a special sort of irony I am talking about; for reasons that will be clear later, I'll call it 'free irony'. It is not the irony of a person who says something other than what her words mean literally, and whose intended message depends upon and exploits the literal meaning. Instead it is the irony of a person who says something other than what her words mean to Clarissa and her colluders. Her message depends upon and exploits the meaning it has for them.

Bertha's statements cannot be understood apart from this 'other-than' quality. This is because the word 'suffers' has been appropriated by people like Clarissa. They have learned how to use this word in the truly naturalistic cases, as when a person is said to suffer from migraine or shingles, and by their attitude or emotion they try to approximate such cases. They might be said to 'play off' of the straightforward use of this word. Bertha on the other hand 'plays off' of Clarissa's usage when she speaks of Clarissa's 'suffering'. By this she captures, ironically, all that's going on with Clarissa. No straightforward, 'literal', stand-alone description could accomplish this.

JUDGE: Clarissa, we cannot proceed unless you testify. Tell me, honestly now, wasn't there just a shred of inauthenticity in all this suffering of yours? I mean, compare your attitude toward this situation with how you felt when you were four and your family's pet raccoon was run over by a car. (Yes, we know all about that and a lot of other things too.) Wasn't there some small difference between the suffering you experienced then and now? I use the word 'inauthenticity', but use any word you like, for instance, 'disingenuousness', 'unstraightforwardness', or 'artfulness'. What about it, Clarissa? Honestly now.

CLARISSA: (huffy). I thought you were impartial, and here you are accusing me. Nothing could be plainer, you're calling me a liar. Don't you think it's hard to be as isolated from others as I've been? Why do you want to punish me for it?

DEFENSE ATTORNEY: My client is right, Your Honour. You are asking leading questions.

JUDGE: Hold on a minute. I never said Clarissa was a liar. What I'm talking about isn't like a lie a person tells. It's a lie a person lives. She's all caught up in it.

DEFENSE ATTORNEY: Well then, Clarissa could hardly be expected to answer your question, now could she? If she's been completely caught up in this supposed lie, then for her it's the same as the truth. How can she act as a witness to whether her emotions have been completely honest in this matter?

JUDGE: (defensively, and wiping her brow again). Look here, I'm not the one on the witness stand.

DEFENSE ATTORNEY: I didn't mean to suggest such a thing, Your Honour. I only want to clarify the issues. My point is, if Clarissa is actually living her supposed lie, then for her it's the same as the truth, isn't it?

JUDGE: Yes, well, I suppose so.

DEFENSE ATTORNEY: So for all you know, you're living a lie just as much as you say she is.

JUDGE: Come, come, my good fellow, don't you think you're pushing things a bit far?

DEFENSE ATTORNEY: That's precisely the question we have to ask you, Your Honour. Isn't that right, Clarissa?

CLARISSA: That's right, Your Honour. I'm just as sincere as you are. Maybe more.

Clarissa's colluders, pro and con, agree on this: she was either cynically mendacious or straightforwardly caring. But for Bertha, these views are complementary, and make up a single falsifying perspective on the situation, a dyad of options both of which are false. Though her view is independent of both, her expression of that view, which is unambiguous for her, can always be construed to support either of these complementary positions. There is a perpetual possibility that what she says will mean something different to her hearers, and it is because of this that I call Bertha's report ironic.

So free irony is possible only because self-deception consists in an artificially delimited set of interpretations of self-deception itself, which set excludes the ironical view. It is possible only because apparently identical lexical resources can be appropriated into these two rival contexts of understanding. The rival contexts seem at once to be both correlative and incommensurable, in the way that the competing construals of certain optical illusions are both correlative and incommensurable. Each construal depends upon the possibility of the other, yet there is no possibility of any construal of either that will render then simultaneously apparent.

THE SIMPLICITY OF FREE IRONY

As ordinarily understood irony is contrasted with literalness. In a tone that's ironic in this standard sense, someone might say, "It's kind of Clarissa to invite us to her evenings at home, when we are so far below her socially". This a non-literal way of saying what would literally be said by, "Clarissa is condescending." A failure to appreciate a standard irony is naivete or gullibility, as when father comes in from a pouring rain and exclaims, "I'm sure glad it didn't rain today!" and his four-year-old says, "But Daddy, it is raining and look how wet you are!" But the incongruity that constitutes free irony is not the incongruity between what Bertha says and literalness. It is an incongruity between what she says and what Clarissa and her colluders understand. It is an incongruity of outlooks or mentalities.

Whereas the father who came in from the rain was being ironic relative to what he himself would say *if he were* being straightforward, Bertha is ironic because she is straightforward. It would be incorrect to say his is an intended irony while hers is not, for she appreciates all along the way she is being misunderstood. The father's irony is founded in a comprehension of a literal construal of the sentence he is uttering, relative to what he wants to say by means of it. Bertha's irony on the other hand is founded in a comprehension of what self-deceivers and their colluders will understand of her utterance, relative to what she wants to say by means of it. His irony is internal to the circle of discourse in which all fully competent speakers participate; hers is a manifestation of a disparity of outlooks that divides speakers and fractures the circle.

In the standard, simplistic view of irony, an ironical act consists of (a) a surface or literal meaning that fits poorly with the context, (b) an intended meaning that fits well with the context, and (c) an intention that the intended respondent(s) appreciate the incongruity of (a), the surface or literal meaning in its context and also appreciate (b), the intended meaning. In other words, the incongruity of literal meaning and context is intended to be taken as a clue to the inappropriateness of taking that meaning at face value. It is intended to be taken as a clue that 'beneath' a surface meaning there operates a core intended meaning.

Clearly, on this view there is in irony a conjunction of two non-ironic or literal elements, the surface meaning and the core intention. The ironic act is internally complex; a process is presumed, which leads from intended meaning to ironic expression. But with free irony there is no internal complexity because there is no intended meaning separate from its expression. In standard irony, the ironist's intention can in principle always be given a non-ironic expression, i.e. a literal translation. But in free irony this is not possible; the ironic meaning of the act cannot be captured by a non-ironic paraphrase. I'd like to show this by the following story.

The college trustees authorized a statue of himself that a benefactor stipulated be erected as a condition of his contribution. The irony of the action was of course lost on those faculty members who complained about honouring a low-brow entrepreneur rather than a high-minded scholar. But the trustees in this case fully appreciated the fact that genuinely high-minded scholars work for less petty and more enduring ends than the 'honour' they were bestowing on this occasion, and that those who seek such an honour—the exhibition of their images in public places—have, as Jesus said, their reward. By the act of authorizing the image of the benefactor, the board satisfied him by granting him the lesser part.

The trustees' action was freely ironic. This means that what they intended could *not* be separated from what they did. The irony of their action was no quaint cosmetic feature of it, but essential to it. Their attitude toward the benefactor could not have been expressed by a 'literal' statement, however carefully qualified, or by a statue that subtly but irreverently caricatured him in a manner that emphasized his crassness. Their attitude couldn't have been more directly expressed in either of these ways because they meant neither to praise nor to mock, but something different from both, something achievable only by commissioning a first-class piece of statuary as requested, which is to say, something not achievable without this irony. Nor is the trustees' intent beneath the observable surface of what they did; it was indissociable from what could be observed.

To appreciate this, suppose that in an insecure moment

(after being subjected to the wrath of the faculty for a few weeks) they decide to issue a statement 'literally' setting forth their intent so that no one can misunderstand. They might, for example, say that "with the most notable sort of recognition that can be drawn from a domain of dubious recognitions, we are duly and fittingly acknowledging the most notable sort of deed that can be drawn from the domain of deeds of dubious value." But this will not do. It does not in fact duly and fittingly acknowledge the deed, but instead withholds the due and fitting acknowledgement. It does not actually express the trustees' regard for the deed in a manner appropriate to the deed. The meaning of the original act is lost. For the trustees meant no insult, not even a faint or comic one, and they did not naively intend to place the benefactor's achievements on any scale appropriate for measuring the worth of purely motivated humanitarian work. Their act was to render if not to Caesar then to Rockefeller all that was his due. It was a just and appropriate act rather than a sardonic one, and if I seem to be speaking ironically in saying this then I am speaking well.

So the supposed core meaning of the ironic act—its meaning apart from the supposed outward conduct—does not exist as such. By the same token, their act's surface meaning— its meaning apart from a supposed core intention—does not exist as such either. Now there is a misunderstanding of free irony that is an analogue of collusion. It consists in this: The observer of the ironist is in collusion with whatever self-deceiver(s) the ironist is responding to. This colluding perception systematically prevents the observer from comprehending the ironist's comprehending response to the self-deceiver. I'll call this uncomprehending, self-deceived construal a 'reduction of free irony'.

Imagine an observer who is misreading the trustees' action as a gullible exaltation of the very kind of unreflective dedication to petty affairs that the college stands against. Now imagine further that this observer learns more about the trustees—discovers, for example, evidence of their appreciation for scholarship and the reflective life generally. This discovery might well lead him to suppose that while his initial judgment had accurately captured the truth about their outward behaviour, the behaviour itself had mislead him. Now, he thinks, he is able by a revisionary judgment to see beneath this surface to their 'real' corporate intent, which seems to him a determination surreptitiously to ridicule this man who thinks they would prostitute themselves, but who naively or stupidly has not anticipated (and will no doubt never suspect) what comic weapons they can wield, weapons that will be appreciated by the cognescenti.

This newly 'enlightened' observer will have attributed his 'mistake' to a misleading quality of the trustees' conduct. He will suppose he has been duped not by himself but by them, or at least by their conduct. Any irony he ascribes to this conduct will be of the simplistic sort exemplified by "I'm sure glad it didn't rain today!" in the example mentioned earlier.

Compare to this the analogous ascription of a malicious core intention that a newcomer might make to Clarissa. After early observations the newcomer might cease thinking of Clarissa's aloofness as a sign of dignified solitude and wonder whether, 'down deep', she might be haughty or afraid. An observer's reduction of freely ironic conduct and 'construction' of what he thinks is its literal meaning is like this colluding newcomer's reading of self-deceptive conduct and his 'construction' of what he thinks is its real intent. Both are falsifications.

I conclude that only the free ironist perceives either self-deceivers or other free ironists for what they are. For only she can see what is manifest in the observable conduct. She alone avoids the error of looking for a meaning underlying this conduct, and for a self to intend this meaning. For example, if Clarissa were actually a completely caring person, that fact would be apparent to the free ironist even if Clarissa were also shy and modest. A free ironist will observe the demeanour of a woman whose attitude toward others is a superior one, not a woman who is superior in her attitude. The difference is stark; it is the difference between self-forgetfulness and self-involvement. In the case of the actual Clarissa, the free ironist would not have observed a person who is superior in refinement, sensitivity, and culture, as she made herself out to be, but a person who was making herself out to be one who is superior in these ways. And again, the difference between these two kinds of conduct, though lost on Clarissa and her colluders, is stark and obvious, and I cannot but suppose that we all have experience in perceiving this difference.

Is the account I have given of person perception behaviouristic? Yes, but not in the standard sense. Though everything that can be known about another's conduct is indeed observable, it is not exoterically available; all normal observers cannot make the observations. A moral condition governs other-perception, namely, that the observer not be a self-deceiver in virtue of colluding with the self-deceiver he is observing, and therefore that he neither exonerates the self-deceiver nor condemns him. Therefore, no science can be erected on the foundation of this kind of behaviourism. In addition, what I have concluded supports also the *Geisteswissenschaftliche* doctrine of *Verstehen*, but in a severely compromised fashion. For though it implies that it is by a direct understanding and not by an inference to an explanation that we comprehend the behaviour of others, that understanding depends not at all on an empathic identification with or divination of the mental life of another; to see the behaviour ironically is to perceive in it all the agent's relevant mentation.

To understand others one must be part of their community, or place oneself in community with them. A necessary condition for achieving the required kind of community, for empathy rather than accusation or exoneration, is to be unself-deceived oneself, which means at least, as we have seen, to be free of self-justifying concerns and correlative accusing attitudes toward others. Understanding others' conduct is itself a moral kind of conduct.

Like the colluders we've discussed, social science has operated in the fiction that all this is not so. This is the fiction that we can discount the role of personal integrity, or lack of it, and achieve an ordering of 'knowledge' that can be spread out explicitly in talk or texts and mechanically shared with one another—as if knowledge were a commodity and learning an acquisition. This is the fiction that there is something of human conduct, including speech, that underlies its observable surface and is its 'meaning', and that we possess a cognitive capacity to grasp that meaning, perhaps by analogy to our own inner intention of meaning (and we are supposed to be able to grasp our own intention directly, whereas this supposed intention and this supposed direct intuition are also fictional). Integral to this fiction is the idea that understanding another person is a matter of drawing an inference on the basis of external clues. Physiognomic recognition has no part in what many behavioural and social scientists think we do when we apprehend the social realities in which we participate.

Oliver Sacks makes certain conjectures about his own discipline in the light of Dr P's illness, which I described earlier, just as I have made certain conjectures about work in self-deception theory in the light of Clarissa's conduct. He sees neurology itself as suffering from a kind of agnosia, and his remarks may be applied to self-deception theory to the same extent that agnosia may be seen as analogous to self-deception.

> "For classical neurology (like classical physics) has always been mechanical—from Hughlings Jackson's mechanical analogies to the computer analogies of today... But our mental

processes, which constitute our being and life, are not just abstract and mechanical, but personal, as well.... And if this is missing, we become computer-like, as Dr P. was. And, by the same token, if we delete the...personal from the cognitive sciences, we reduce them to something as defective as Dr P.—and we reduce our apprehension of the concrete and real." [4]

By a sort of comic and awful analogy, our current cognitive neurology and psychology resembles nothing so much as poor Dr P.! We need the concrete and real, as he did; and we fail to see this, as he failed to see it. Our cognitive sciences are themselves suffering from an agnosia essentially similar to Dr P.'s.

THE FREE IRONIST'S EQUANIMITY

What astounds me about the free ironist is his willingness non-collusively to live with the perpetual possibility of being misunderstood. In speaking and acting straightforwardly, Bertha and the trustees made no attempt to control others' interpretations of their conduct. If it was not unawares that they let this opportunity go, then they let it go with equanimity.

It could not have been otherwise. If they had not done so, they would have lost their cognitive gift; they would have forfeited their understanding. Recall the imagined effort of the trustees to clarify their intentions. Had they actually tried to do this they would have reduced their irony to collusion. They would have lost their ironic understanding.

The distinction between dramatic and personal irony is preserved here. The straightforward acts of a merely naive person can be misunderstood by people whilst that person is unaware of their misunderstanding. But the personally ironic

4 Ibid., pp. 18-19

free ironist comprehends the possibilities of interpretive abuse and does not resist this evil. Irony, at least of the free kind we are studying here, is virtue's tribute to vice. Ironically, perhaps, only by giving others the freedom to misuse one, can one be free of colluding with them if they do misuse one. In trying by rhetorical control to prevent this misuse one colludes in it.[5]

Are there actually any completely free ironists? Or is it an ideal type I am describing? My answer is that even though it may be an ideal type, there are individuals who approximate that type far more closely than most of us. And I think they will usually be very ordinary and perhaps even unprepossessing sort of people, like the individual Kierkegaard called 'the knight of faith'. They may be mothers or shopkeepers or secretaries whose only distinguishing characteristic is that they don't indulge in taking offense: they are not morally or socially insecure. When someone does what others in their situation would find offensive, they see it for what it is, a major or minor tragedy in the life of the offender. Neither are they manipulative, manipulation being a technique for inducing or forestalling offense which is itself offensive to any insecure person sensitive to the demeaning message in it. Unengaged in emotional self-protection, they have a certain fearlessness about them which usually goes unnoticed because it does not advertise itself as such.

THE FREE IRONIST'S CREATIVITY

I might be understood as saying that Bertha's abandonment of irony would come at the point when she made any attempt to manipulate others into adopting her own understanding of her testimony. But though true, this account is too weak. The stronger account is this: Bertha would abandon her

---

5 There are exceptions to this rule, as when Paul took care not to be thought to be eating meat by certain of his fellow Christians, in fear that it would wound their consciences, since they believed it wrong to eat meat and might be encouraged by his example to violate their moral commitments. In such a case, however, Paul wouldn't have been concerned for his own sake about the possibility of others misconstruing his conduct, but instead for their sakes.

irony whenever she supposed her own interpretation definitive. With this thought she would deceive herself; she would take a reductive view of her own ironic conduct and so abandon it. To be ironical in the moral domain which we are considering is to claim no superiority in one's understanding of the meaning of one's own actions. It is, even in the realm of self-understanding, to be tentative, open, and available for surprise.

I think this point has implications for the expressive power and creativity of the incongruous form in which free ironies are expressed. That form is not, as in self-deception and collusion with self-deception, an instrument by which meaning is delimited, but instead an instrument with which endless possibilities of meaning are opened up. Socrates said, "I alone am wise, because I alone know that I know nothing." By this he conveyed to those with ears to hear neither that he was wise nor that he was foolish nor any other determinately expressible idea. His way of laying claim to wisdom alters our understanding of wisdom. It brings to bear multiple implications concerning both knowledge and wisdom and the pomposity of the claim men make to possess either or both of them. Wisdom becomes, by his utterance, something multiply illustrated, incongruously suspended as it were between considerations of knowledge, good judgment, sagacity, etc., on one hand, and, on the other, the sense of the impossibility of any of these achievements.

So with the trustees. Their gift can be construed in many different ways; and it is what it is—inexhaustible in its suggestions of tolerance, insight, compassion, and unsentimentality—precisely because it can so easily be understood to be naive and just as easily to be insulting. These interpretations are not alternatives to some supposed definitive account telling us "what, in actuality, the trustees meant"; instead, the fact that these interpretations of the trustees' action are possible *is part of what their action means.* If the benefactor and his colluders can be flattered or offended by the trustees' gift—that is what makes it ironical.

The utterance of Socrates and the decision of the trustees are of an order different from the self-deceiver's self-presentations. They are self-forgetful rather than self-conscious. Socrates' utterance opened itself to reconstrual in terms of successive expansions of contexts or perspectives he himself invoked by the incongruity he exploited. Some of these construals he might have anticipated; others not. However, he precluded none of them; indeed, I like to think that he invited them. For him to learn that he provided evidence to the self-deceivers of Athens that they were justified in their treatment of him would have been, and was, an increase in his self-understanding.

What Socrates said can never be all that it is if construed wholly in terms of a single context or perspective. This is not its deficiency but its power. His utterance refracted not a limited and determinate "inner" intention but the confluence of many dimensions and levels of the social world. Meaning is a perennial bloom in the linguistic space defined by speakers in community; it is not bound by any discrete linguistic unit such as a word, a sentence, a paragraph, or a text. Meaning is social in the sense that interpretation is a corporate activity that in ordinary life is never completed or definitive.

It is because the free ironist conceals nothing that he is often thought not to take himself seriously. He may not know what he thinks until he hears what he has to say, and he increases in his understanding of what he meant by observing others' responses. Yet because he is not colluding with them he does not feel victimized by those responses; they do not define for him what he is. He does not need them to validate an effort on his part to establish a particular conception of himself because that is not an enterprise he is engaged in. So he is free to allow himself to be revealed in what he says.

It is for all these reasons that I consider a freely ironical act novel, and hence creative, whereas the self-deceiver's contrivance of a determinate personality is artful and drearily repeatable, no matter how 'original' he tries to be. The ironist invites uncoerced and self-expressive response from others, whereas the self-deceiver is a manipulator, extorting, if he can, a certain predictable range of stylized responses predefined as those that will validate the lie he is living.